"Charlie Hawkins has diagnosed the problems of 'sick' meetings insightfully and accurately. Even more important, his easy-to-understand prescriptions are totally realistic. It's a terrific guide to having more productive and more personally satisfying meetings."

—Robert J. Savard, Savard Consulting, Inc.

"[Make Meetings Matter] provides detailed and on-target direction for all those who have hosted or suffered through meetings that never seemed to get where they were going or never seemed to be headed anywhere in the first place. It's the next best thing to having Charlie facilitate your meeting in person."

—A.C. Croft, management consultant, author of
Managing a Public Relations Firm for Growth and Profit

"*Make Meetings Matter* gives you the roadmap to blow out the cobwebs from time-wasting, tedious meetings. Every chapter has gems of wisdom and practical advice to brighten up and shorten your meetings, while getting more done."

—Jennifer Cowan, Sr. Process Saftey Engineer,
Process Saftey & Reliability Group

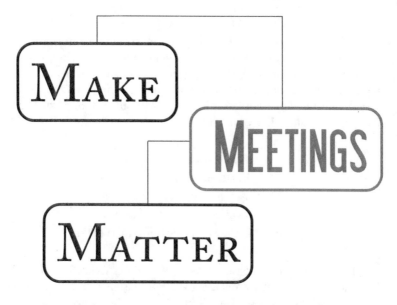

MAKE MEETINGS MATTER

BAN BOREDOM, CONTROL CONFUSION, AND TERMINATE TIME-WASTING

⇨ Get More Done in Less Time With Less Work

⇨ Keep Participants Engaged and Energized

⇨ Embrace Nontraditional Meetings Using New Technologies

CHARLIE HAWKINS

CAREER PRESS

THE CAREER PRESS, INC.
FRANKLIN LAKES, NJ

MAKE MEETINGS MATTER
EDITED BY KATE HENCHES
TYPESET BY MICHAEL FITZGIBBON
Cover design by Jeff Piasky
Printed in the U.S.A. by Book-mart Press

To order this title, please call toll-free 1-800-CAREER-1 (NJ and Canada: 201-848-0310) to order using VISA or MasterCard, or for further information on books from Career Press.

The Career Press, Inc., 3 Tice Road, PO Box 687,
Franklin Lakes, NJ 07417
www.careerpress.com

Library of Congress Cataloging-in-Publication Data
Hawkins, Charlie.
    Make meetings matter : ban boredom, control confusion, and eliminate time-wasting / by Charlie Hawkins
        p. cm.
    Includes index.
    ISBN 978-1-60163-015-5
1. Business meetings—Planning. 2. Meetings—Planning. 3. Group facilitation. I. Title.

HF5734.5.H39 2008
65.4'56—dc22

2008005646

Acknowledgments

In a real sense, every meeting that I have attended, initiated, facilitated, or observed during the past four decades is part of the fabric of *Make Meetings Matter*. There have been some truly memorable meetings and several unmitigated disasters, with most falling somewhere in between.

Participants in my meetings skills workshops have freely shared strategies and practices that have contributed to successful meetings, along with many examples of things to avoid.

My wife and best friend, Alicia, was my main encourager throughout the process. Her gentle reminders to make time for writing helped me stay on track in the midst of many other priorities. The many contributors to my previous book, *First Aid for Meetings*, helped lay the groundwork for this book.

I am privileged to work with several groups of business owners and key executives as a chair for Vistage International. Our monthly meetings have given me a living laboratory to test out ideas and to truly deliver meetings that matter.

Finally, thanks to the fine team at Career Press for bringing this project to life.

Thanks to you, one and all.

Charlie Hawkins

CONTENTS

Part III: At the End and After the Meeting: The 4 C's of Completion   133

Part IV: Additional Strategies and Solutions   179

Appendix   203

Index   213

About the Author   221

INTRODUCTION

LET'S HAVE A MEETING

If those familiar words make you shudder, you are not alone. Meetings should drive results—instead, they drive most people crazy! Meetings, in many organizations, have earned a reputation as time-wasters and energy-drainers, and it is a wonder that anything at all gets accomplished at certain meetings. It seems that few organizations are immune: businesses of all sizes, associations, professional groups, government, academic institutions, hospitals, churches, volunteer organizations, and clubs center many of their activities around meetings.

When meetings are effective, the potential for results is unlimited; participants feel energized and valued. They contribute freely, find solutions, and make decisions. Things get done. Meetings take many forms, from small staff meetings, phone conferences, and board meetings to brainstorming sessions and training Webinars involving dozens of people. Meetings are a fact of life around the world.

Yet, many—if not most—meetings are dysfunctional in some way. Some are tedious and boring, seldom staying focused. Many people confide that they are reluctant to volunteer for committees or boards, simply because the meetings are so long and tiresome. Some groups follow the same routine, meeting after meeting, seemingly going nowhere. Most of us rightly consider meetings a monumental waste of time—they simply don't matter. Still other meetings leave people "wounded" or manipulated in some way, because the meeting initiator or other participants discount or squash their ideas. Perhaps they are victims to hidden agendas. After such meetings, people leave feeling drained and often angry. Some groups follow the same routine, meeting after meeting, seemingly going nowhere.

Is there a better way? Happily, the answer is yes.

When meetings are effective, the potential for results is virtually un-limited. In meetings that matter, participants feel energized and valued. They contribute freely, find solutions, and make decisions. Things get done, less time is spent, and there is clear follow-up. There is a huge payoff for "getting it right," because meetings have an enormous poten-tial for effective collaboration.

My contention is that most people would like to change the way they "do" meetings, but don't know how. After planning, facilitating, observ-ing, and participating in thousands of meetings during a 35-year business and consulting career, I have seen dramatic improvement in meetings when participants understand and practice a few basic skills. Even more encour-aging is the news that anyone—and any group—can learn and implement these techniques with relatively little effort.

Make Meetings Matter does not provide a rigid model or format for meetings; nor does it suggest that there is only one "right way" to run meetings. In fact, there are many right ways to run meetings. However, the strategies and techniques in this book will point you in the right direction, and show you how even small changes can make a big difference in any meeting you initiate, lead, or attend. As you try a few of the ideas and experiment with others, you'll gradually develop some healthy options for your organization's meetings. Who knows, you might even grow to look forward to meetings!

Who Should Read This Book?

Anyone who leads, facilitates, presents, or participates in small group meetings (from two to 25 people) can benefit from the tools and ideas in *Make Meetings Matter.* Although many of the techniques and skills also apply to larger groups, this book concentrates on the small- to medium-sized meetings that are the norm for most organizations.

Twenty-first century technology has made a significant impact on the ability to conduct meetings. Tools are available to enable meeting initiators and facilitators design better agendas, invite people easily, involve people in remote locations, and follow up effectively. Although you will find references to hardware, software, and Internet tools throughout the book, Chapter 14 is devoted specifically to technology-enabled meetings.

I once thought that business meetings were different from meetings in other groups such as schools and colleges, churches, clubs, and volunteer organizations. In some respects, they are quite different, especially when group members are volunteers rather than employees. Through the years, however, I've learned that there are more similarities than differences. People are people. After all, many of the same people who meet in volunteer groups also participate in business meetings. If you fall in one of the following groups, you will find something of value in these pages.

MEDIUM AND LARGE BUSINESS ORGANIZATIONS

Directors, executives, managers, department heads, team leaders, committee or sub-committee heads, internal consultants, supervisors, trainers, administrative assistants, board members, meeting planners, team members, task force, and committee members.

Small Businesses

Owners, executives, board members, managers, supervisors, team leaders, and all employees who plan, lead, facilitate, or attend meetings.

Volunteer and Nonprofit Groups

Executives, staff, full-time or part-time trainers, committee heads, board members, and volunteers who attend trainings or other meetings.

Hospitals and Healthcare Industries

Chiefs of staff, administrators, board members, department heads, chief/attending surgeons, residents, supervisors, nurses, staff personnel, and committee members.

Academic Institutions

Superintendents, school board members, principals, deans, administrators, department heads, professors, teachers, instructors, counselors, staff support, and PTA leaders.

Consultants

Trainers, planners, strategists, facilitators, subject matter experts, and general or specialized consultants.

Professionals and Professional Associations

Doctors, lawyers, accountants, architects, consulting engineers, and staff support personnel.

Churches/Religious Institutions

Clergy, staff, board chairs, officers and members, deacons, committee leaders and members, and administrators.

Clubs and Associations

Officers, committee members and chairs, staff support people, program planners, and members who plan or attend meetings.

Meeting Roles

Chapters 2 and 4 detail some basic meeting roles and responsibilities that may be a little different than those with which you are familiar. Here is a brief recap:

⇨ The *initiator* is the person who calls the meeting. He/she generally "owns" the problem or issue, and is ultimately responsible for the outcome. This personal is often the nominal or actual group leader.

⇨ A *facilitator* is anyone who serves as the process leader for a meeting, helping *participants* to stay on track, work within time parameters, and bring things to a conclusion.

⇨ The *timekeeper* assists the facilitator and the group by reminding them of beginning and ending time for the meeting and individual parts.

⇨ *Resource people* provide input and expertise for a group.

⇨ *Participants* are the main players in a meeting. They share information and input, contribute ideas, analyze issues, make decisions, and generally contribute to achieving the meeting's purpose.

My hope is that you will use this resource to make your meetings matter.

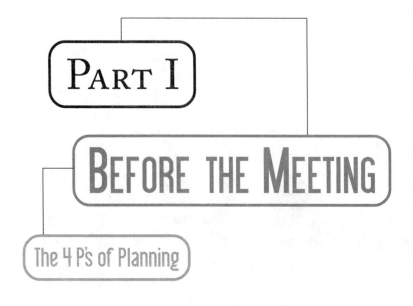

Part I

Before the Meeting

The 4 P's of Planning

Purpose

Establish and communicate a clear purpose and expected outcomes for your meeting. Determine if a meeting is really necessary.

People

Decide on the people who will attend based on whether they can help achieve the purpose. Clarify the roles of each participant.

Place

Select the right location, meeting space, and room set-up to accomplish your purpose.

Preparation

Select the most important content items to be discussed, solved, or decided and prepare an agenda; then, plan the process, give participants advance materials, and handle logistics arrangements.

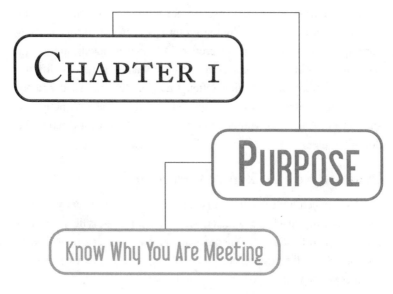

CHAPTER I

PURPOSE

Know Why You Are Meeting

The Truth You Never Hear

"Well, uh, it's about 10 after, so let's go ahead and start the staff meeting. As usual, we're, um, not really sure why we're meeting, except that, well, we always meet on Mondays. Oh, I think Sam's got something to report on the southern region. Anytime you think of something, speak up, even if it is off the subject, and you interrupt someone else. Uh, we'll keep going until we run out of steam, and we'll all probably be frustrated when we end, because we will have wasted a lot of time without accomplishing anything."

The Challenges

No Purpose Defined or Unclear Purpose

When the purpose of a meeting is not stated or is unclear, people often find themselves in the midst of a discussion that is irrelevant to them. Without a purpose, meetings can flounder, turning into a forum for discussing anything that pops into participants' minds. Starting a meeting without a purpose is like starting a journey without a specific destination in mind. If it is not clear why the group has been called together, few participants will know how to prepare. Without a stated purpose, the meeting may start with vague comments and wander in several different directions before finally ending. Often, little gets accomplished, and participants are frustrated at having wasted so much time with nothing to show for it. A meeting without a purpose is likely to be a meeting that doesn't matter.

Purpose Not Linked to Outcomes

Even when a clear purpose is established (and especially when it isn't!) a meeting that lacks expected outcomes, or results, is likely to end in confusion and frustration. Outcomes are a means to measure whether or not you achieve the meeting purpose. Without them, you may never know whether you have achieved the purpose or not.

"Things were fine, until we started having meetings."

Purpose

The Trap of Regularly Scheduled Meetings

Regularly scheduled meetings are often convened without having a definite purpose or expected outcome. Almost every organization with which I have been associated has held daily, weekly, or monthly staff meetings. These meetings occur at the executive level, in most mid-level departments, and at the operating level. Often staff and committee meetings become institutionalized, and continue to be called whether or not they are really necessary. Athough regularly scheduled meetings tend to follow a set format (for example, each department head reports, old business/new business, and so on), the purpose of these meetings is seldom questioned, or even known.

Paragon Cleaning Products was a successful medium-size company that manufactured industrial cleaning products. Every Wednesday without fail, the 11-member operating staff attended a luncheon meeting at a nearby restaurant. Every staff member was expected to have something prepared to say or present to the other members.

There was no set format for the presentations. Seth, the head of operations, usually recited a laundry list of problems his department was experiencing, in his whining tone of voice. Joe, the controller, talked about deals going down and the status of the financial markets—Joe always brought along a couple of charts, which few people could comprehend. Agnes, who ran the marketing department, would often talk about a new advertising or promotion campaign about to break, or other activities such as market research. Woody, who was head of international sales, usually shared some outrageous stories about taking a 36-hour trip to Nairobi for a two-hour meeting.

And so it went. The food was good, the camaraderie was great, and nothing was ever discussed that made much of a difference. The meetings started at noon, and seldom finished before 2 p.m., often running much longer. The president never fixed a purpose for these luncheons, and no one on the operating committee seemed to know the reason for the meetings. It seemed as if the main purpose was social. If so, many people wasted a lot of hours preparing presentations of little interest to anyone else. Important decisions of Paragon Cleaning Products were seldom made at the weekly meetings. These meetings really did not matter.

Strategies and Solutions for Purposeful Meetings

⇨ Determine as precisely as possible the purpose of the meeting—why you are having the meeting.

⇨ Decide specific outcomes that you want to achieve.

⇨ Don't initiate a meeting when other alternatives may work better.

⇨ Consider holding an asynchronous meeting.

⇨ Communicate the purpose to all who are invited to attend.

⇨ As a participant, ask the initiator to clarify the purpose of a meeting, if it has not been clearly communicated.

⇨ Avoid ulterior purposes and hidden agendas.

⇨ Try a "MOM and POP" approach to planning meetings.

Determine the Purpose of the Meeting

If you are the initiator, the starting point to determine the purpose is to ask: Why are you convening a meeting? What is it you really want to accomplish? What specific outcomes, or results, do you want to achieve?

Some of the more common purposes for different types of meetings are:

Give and receive information—announcements, results, status reports, committee reports, and presentations on subjects of interest to participants; may include reactions and feedback from participants. Types of meetings with this purpose might include:

Purpose

⇨ Staff meetings, committee meetings.

⇨ Project status reports and updates.

⇨ Sales meetings.

⇨ Marketing and sales presentations.

Coordinate—projects, calendars, and assignments.

⇨ Department heads or committee meetings.

⇨ Team or task force meetings.

Learn—skills, procedures, or operations.

⇨ Training meetings and seminars.

⇨ New employee orientation meetings.

⇨ Team training.

⇨ Professional organizations, club meetings, and study groups.

Plan—establish a vision, set goals, determine objectives, and develop strategies.

⇨ Board, team, or departmental retreats.

⇨ Cross-functional team meetings.

⇨ Newly formed groups.

⇨ Planning for major presentations or events.

Solve problems or create opportunities—analyze issues, generate ideas, alternatives, and possible solutions.

⇨ Adhoc groups or task forces formed to address specific situations such as employee absenteeism, or generate funds for a new building.

⇨ Functional teams.

⇨ Committees, boards, and departmental groups.

Decide—evaluate, prioritize, and select options, come to a decision by voting or consensus, assign action steps.

⇨ Groups that generate ideas or solve problems.

⇨ Any group that is presented with alternatives developed by others.

Socialize—get to know one another, and network.

⇨ Groups specifically designed to foster networking, such as clubs and associations.

⇨ Often a valuable component of meetings called for other purposes.

Build teamwork—create trust, inspire, motivate, and celebrate success.

⇨ A useful purpose for teams or groups that are forming.

⇨ Meetings to announce and celebrate successful results or high achievers.

Multiple-purpose meetings—may consist of some reporting, problem-solving, and decision-making.

⇨ This is common in staff meetings, boards, committees, and groups that meet on a regular basis.

From this list, it is obvious that people hold meetings for many different reasons. Being clear about the purpose is the foundation for having a meeting that matters. Purpose statements should be as specific as possible. Here are some sample purpose statements:

⇨ Review fourth quarter results by region and take action on under-performing regions.

⇨ Report and react to status of key projects and decide to reallocate resources as necessary.

⇨ Learn new features of new software program.

⇨ Reach agreement on top three candidates for project engineer position.

⇨ Generate ideas for fund-raising alternatives.

⇨ Introduce new team members and clarify work assignments.

Notice that each of the purpose statements starts with a verb, followed by a specific object. Stay away from vague purposes or purposes with only adjectives and nouns, such as "project review" or "team brainstorming." Instead, be specific, such as "generate ideas for warehouse storage solution," or "decide on funds for Sussex project."

Purpose

DECIDE THE SPECIFIC OUTCOMES
YOU WANT TO ACHIEVE

Outcomes are specific, measurable results that you want to reach in the meeting. For example, if the purpose is stated as "decide on concepts to present to management," an outcome might be "agree on three concepts that meet our criteria." If the purpose is to learn the features of a new software program, an outcome might be "demonstrate ability to download data from server to desktop computers." Such outcomes are specific and measurable. When you achieve them, you know you have accomplished the stated purpose.

Not all purposes can be evaluated by achieving specific outcomes. This is especially true if the purpose is something softer, such as networking or team building, or if the outcomes will be played out throughout a period of time. Let's say you have completed an in-house survey that indicates your employee morale is low. You decide to initiate a meeting, with the stated purpose to "generate ideas for improving employee morale." Although the ultimate outcome might be to eventually improve morale by X percent, as indicated by a follow-up survey, it would be impossible to know whether you will have achieved this outcome at the end of the meeting. All you can do is generate ideas and options that you *hope* will eventually achieve that outcome. In such cases, limit the meeting outcome to what can actually be accomplished in the meeting itself. For example, "generate ideas for two to three department-level initiatives to test during the third quarter."

Take a moment now to reflect on a recent meeting you have initiated or attended. Was the purpose clear? Was everyone attending aware of the purpose? Were specific outcomes attached to the purpose?

Making an agenda is much easier when you have spent some time getting clear on the meeting's purpose and anticipated outcomes. Agenda preparation will be covered in detail in Chapter 4.

DON'T INITIATE A MEETING WHEN OTHER ALTERNATIVES MAY WORK BETTER

Many meetings are held out of habit or impulse—the "we always meet on Wednesday morning" syndrome. The least productive meetings are ones where the goals can be accomplished in another less-costly and time-consuming way. Here are some questions to ask to discover if a meeting is really necessary:

⇨ What would be gained or lost if the meeting were not held?

⇨ Can the purpose be accomplished by another means: e-mail, one-on-one conference, or phone?

⇨ Can you achieve the same outcomes by holding an asynchronous meeting vs. a live face-to-face meeting (see below)?

⇨ If you hold regular staff or committee meetings, consider having half as many meetings, such as meeting every other week or month. Use phone messages or e-mails to communicate between meetings.

Other reasons for not holding a meeting:

⇨ When there is not enough time or inadequate data for participants to prepare.

⇨ When your mind is already made up, and you really do not want input or ideas.

⇨ When the subject is confidential, such as personnel issues.

⇨ When the subject is trivial.

CONSIDER HOLDING AN ASYNCHRONOUS MEETING

A *synchronous* meeting occurs in real time, when all participants are meeting together in the same room (face to face), or electronically via the Internet or teleconference connection. At their best, synchronous meetings are an effective way for a group of people to:

Purpose

➯ Collaborate to solve problems, generate ideas, and have robust conversations.

➯ Observe and interpret verbal and physical reactions or levels of commitment (applies to face-to-face and videoconference meetings only).

➯ Communicate information clearly and ensure that everyone understands it.

➯ Celebrate accomplishments, promotions; build team esprit.

➯ Coordinate calendars and priorities (often done more effectively electronically).

➯ Build consensus.

➯ Learn something, and practice skills with peer and instructor feedback.

At their worst, synchronous meetings are:

➯ An expensive waste of an organization's resources.

➯ Exercises in futility where little is accomplished.

➯ A forum for posturing and bravado.

An *asynchronous* meeting occurs during a period of time, with participants "attending" on their own schedules. This concept, although not totally new, has been made much easier because of the Internet. Here's how asynchronous meetings work:

➯ Participants generate information and contribute ideas or opinions when it is convenient for them. Generally, a time window is set.

➯ Ideas, feedback, and comments are posted to a common space such as a Website. Input is then available for others to review, and each contributor is encouraged to build on the input of others. In many respects, a blog is an ongoing, asynchronous meeting.

➯ Someone usually compiles and acts on the information received.

Asynchronous meetings can be very effective ways to generate ideas, provide project updates, "vote" anonymously, or express qualitative opinions on issues. Similar to any meeting, asynchronous, meetings should have a clear purpose and outcome. In the "old days" (pre-Internet), I worked for a company that had an idea room. Anytime someone wanted input, ideas and thought-starters from others, he or she would post the question on the bulletin board in the idea room, and invite contribution. The ideas, usually anonymous, would be gathered after a time, and the results compiled. This early form of asynchronous meetings has given way to Web-based collaboration, which enables participants to easily contribute from anywhere on the planet.

Communicate the Purpose to All Attending

There are few things more disconcerting than being invited to a meeting without knowing what it is all about or why you are there. At the very least, you feel anxious because you are unprepared and don't know what is expected. You may also feel annoyed, because it may cut into other priorities, or you know you could contribute better if you were prepared. In the absence of information, many of us assume the worst—if we are invited to a meeting without knowing the purpose, we start thinking our department is being eliminated or something else equally disastrous.

Of course, there are times when confidentiality or urgency dictates that the purpose not be announced in advance. But most of the time, a little prior information is useful. As the initiator, it is to your advantage to have people come to your meeting with an informed point of view. How will they be able to prepare and fully participate if they don't know what the purpose is?

It is not always necessary, but certainly acceptable, to communicate the expected outcomes in advance—you can also announce them at the beginning of the meeting.

Purpose

Ask the Initiator to Clarify the Purpose

If you are invited to a meeting and the purpose is not clear, simply ask the initiator (the person who calls the meeting) or his or her assistant. This does not have to be a confrontation, simply a request. Knowing the purpose will enable you to prepare in advance, and to determine whether or not it is worth your time to attend, if you have a choice.

Avoid Ulterior Purposes and Hidden Agendas

Ulterior purposes, also known as hidden agendas, are a little tricky. They crop up when you are told you are meeting for one purpose, but there is something else entirely different going on, often quite subtle.

The members of the fund-raising committee for a community volunteer group were frequently asked for ideas. As ideas were offered from committee members, Evelyn, the chair, frequently responded with killer phrases such as, "we'll never get that past the board," and "we tried something like that three years ago and it didn't work."

On the other hand, Evelyn would often present her ideas and then support them enthusiastically. To be fair, some of them were pretty good. The problem was that the only ideas she seemed to support were her own. It wasn't too long before ideas from the rest of the committee members dried up. Then Evelyn began to complain that she was the only one who came up with ideas.

It became clear that Evelyn's ulterior purpose—whether she was aware of it or not—was to elicit the group members' reactions to her ideas. The committee fell apart after several months, with most members feeling unappreciated and manipulated. Evelyn complained about how hard it was to get volunteers to serve on committees, never suspecting she may have been part of the problem.

As a meeting initiator, the best way to avoid ulterior purposes is to honestly examine what you really want to accomplish, and to let everyone know what that is. If you simply want to get reactions to your ideas, just say so. Having established this purpose, you also need to set the climate for honest evaluation and feedback. If all you want is positive feedback, why hold a meeting? Few things diminish group members more than to be told their ideas are wanted, only to have them systematically judged or dismissed by a meeting initiator who really does not want input from others. These are truly meetings that do not matter. Sadly, like the emperor from the fairy tale, initiators are not always aware of what they are doing, though it is transparent to everyone else.

As a participant, you may be able to pick up ulterior motives by comparing what the initiator says to what he or she does. If your and other participants' ideas are systematically dismissed, there may an ulterior motive to the meeting, or at least a very negative boss! Unfortunately, there is a little you can do in most situations, except to find a reason to skip the next meeting.

Another ulterior—or at least unstated—purpose of some meetings is to evaluate people, especially when the meeting initiator (a manager or supervisor) is convening with subordinates. The meeting becomes a show-case to see how employees perform under pressure. Certainly, anyone who makes a presentation to a group is under pressure, especially if they are new at it. More subtly, people are also evaluated according to the quantity and quality of their contributions. Whether meeting initiators acknowledge it or not, the fact is that meetings may be the most visible forum for many people. In some cases, it may be the only time a manager sees an employee or member "in action."

A possible solution to this situation is for managers and supervisors to get to know people outside the meeting environment, thus developing a well-rounded view of how they perform in different situations. Similarly, participants should seek opportunities to meet with their managers one-on-one and in other situations, so that meetings are not a showcase and the only exposure to that employee.

A "MOM AND POP" APPROACH TO PLANNING

In my meeting skills workshops, I recommend taking a MOM and POP approach to meeting planning. These acronyms make it easy to remember the initial steps for effective planning.

MOM stands for "Meeting On the Meeting." The initiator and facilitator—and others if desired—should meet in advance to clarify the purpose and outcomes, decide who should attend, and work up an agenda. This pre-meeting can be brief, and is often done via phone, e-mail, or a brief one-on-one meeting.

POP equates to "Purpose, Outcomes, Plan." The first two are the subject of this chapter. The meeting plan includes selecting who will attend, meeting location, logistics, advance preparation, and the agenda. All of these are included in upcoming chapters.

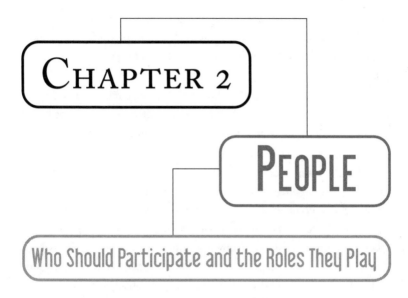

CHAPTER 2

PEOPLE

Who Should Participate and the Roles They Play

The Truth You Never Hear

"I have called the entire staff together, even though most of you won't have a chance to participate, and are not really affected by most of the things we will be discussing or deciding. In reality, this meeting is all about me anyway."

The Challenges

PARTICIPANTS NOT INVOLVED

Has this ever happened to you? You are sitting in a meeting wondering to yourself why in the world you are there. Although the subject is marginally relevant to you, it is something you could read in an e-mail or meeting summary. As the meeting progresses, you "zone out," resorting to doodling on your pad, covertly checking e-mail on your BlackBerry, and imagining all the better things you could be doing rather than wasting time in the meeting. If you are attending a meeting via phone conference or

Internet, the chances for zoning out increase dramatically. It is frustrating to be in a group of several people, and spend most of your time listening to a discussion among two or three people that doesn't involve you or your area of responsibility.

Then there are the "meeting junkies." These people attend meetings because they are curious about what is going on, don't want to be out of the loop, want to be seen, or just don't have anything better to do.

When Carolyn Fisher was a major in the U.S. Air Force, she often attended Department of Defense meetings about upcoming plans for politically sensitive programs. Through time, she noticed that many people who might be involved with these programs at later stages would attend the planning meetings "to see what was happening." As a result, the meetings were often bogged down with questions from people whose involvement was not critical in the planning stage. The meetings ultimately became difficult to manage because of the sheer number of people, and the amount of detailed questions.

KEY PEOPLE ABSENT

The opposite situation occurs when topics of interest to certain people are discussed, and they are not present. Maybe they are on vacation or a business trip, and perhaps the topics surfaced because of issues in other areas. Or maybe the initiator just forgot to invite them. Whatever the reason, things can really get fouled up quickly if people who have a stake in a discussion or decision are not included. The impact of this is usually not apparent until after the meeting, when decisions are second-guessed and agreements unravel.

There is a direct relationship between the people who attend a meeting and the quality of the ideas and decisions that result. When you meet to consider important issues, it is critical that participants representing all sides of the subject are invited. If everyone is of the same mindset, you are going to get predictable, and often ineffective, results. It is similar to having a group of senior managers meet to brainstorm ways to motivate front-line workers without including any lower-level employees in the discussion. For groups that meet often, the phenomenon of groupthink can set in, which can have disastrous results; more about groupthink in Chapter 9.

Roles Not Assigned

Other symptoms of ineffective meetings show up when clear roles have not been assigned to make the meeting run smoothly. As a result, the meeting may easily run off-course, time is not managed well, and the purpose is not accomplished.

Strategies and Solutions for People and Participation

⇨ Get the right people in the room.

⇨ Find ways to include divergent viewpoints when key people are not able to attend.

⇨ In collaborative meetings, keep the group size small.

⇨ Consider having part-time participants.

⇨ If you are invited to a meeting that you feel is only of marginal interest to you or not the best use of your time, ask the initiator if your presence is mandatory. If you choose to stay, use the meeting as a learning opportunity.

⇨ Appoint a facilitator, recorder, and timekeeper to help ensure the meeting functions smoothly.

Get the Right People in the Room

As you consider whom to invite to a meeting, assess the value that each participant can bring to helping achieve the purpose. Is the entire staff required? Do all the committee members need to attend every meeting?

Consider inviting a team (committee, department) representative rather than having the entire group attend. Then ask, have you forgotten to invite anyone whose input or influence would be valuable?

Who should attend a meeting?

⇨ People who can influence or help accomplish the meeting's purpose.

⇨ People who have a stake in the subjects to be covered, especially those who will be affected by decisions made. It is perfectly legitimate to invite people whose attendance would further your purpose, such as getting ideas and recommendations "sold" to higher or different levels.

⇨ People who represent all significant viewpoints on the issue being discussed. It is shortsighted, for example, for a management group to address employee concerns without having the input and opinions of operating-level people.

⇨ People who have critical information to share, such as subject matter experts and people making or participating in presentations.

⇨ Decision-makers or key people whose support is needed for a given decision or agreement to work.

⇨ People to observe the meeting for training or consultation purposes. Be careful to limit the number of "outsiders" attending for this reason.

⇨ People who can make positive contributions, such as problem-solvers, idea generators, astute observers, and experts in the subject area. This may include people from other departments who are really good thinkers.

When I facilitated an idea-generation session for a consumer products company, representatives from the advertising agency were invited to participate. In addition to the account executives and creative team, the agency brought along a person from the media department. I thought this was an unusual choice, as media people usually became involved much later in the process. As it turned out, Bill was one of the most innovative thinkers in the session, and was a terrific contributor to the meeting.

Think twice before inviting:

⇨   People who cannot or are not willing to contribute to accomplishing the meeting's purpose.

⇨   People who are prone to display disruptive behavior in meetings. Chapter 13 lists many such behaviors and how to deal with them. The best way to deal with disruptive people is to not invite them in the first place!

⇨   People who have only a peripheral interest in the subject(s) being covered—if appropriate, send people in this category a copy of the meeting notes or debrief them separately.

⇨   People whose title or temperament would result in them feeling "hurt" if they weren't invited, but have no other valid reason for attending.

FIND WAYS TO INCLUDE DIVERGENT VIEWPOINTS WHEN KEY PEOPLE CANNOT ATTEND

People who are critical to an issue being discussed or decisions being made may not able to attend. If it is clear that their contributions or influence would make a difference in the outcome, consider including them via phone or videoconference, or getting their input prior to the meeting.

A medium-size contractor in New Mexico stages daily huddles, which are stand-up meetings attended by all key managers. The purpose is to review operational priorities and head off any problems. Attendance is mandatory, and if a manager is not able to attend, he or she is expected to join the meeting via phone conference. In more than two years, no one has ever missed a meeting, except for vacations when a representative attends in their place.

With the ability to connect electronically anywhere around the globe, it is relatively easy to have all the key players included in an important meeting. If someone is on vacation, consider postponing the meeting, or get input prior to his or her departure.

In Collaborative Meetings, Keep the Group Size Small

Is there an ideal number of people who should attend a meeting? As a general guideline, a group size of 10 or less is preferable for meetings where a high degree of interaction and collaboration is desired. In my experience, five to eight people is a very workable group size for idea generation, collaborative discussions, and decision-making. When working with larger groups for these types of meetings, break the group down into subgroups for discussion, idea generation, and opinion sharing.

When Major Fisher became the initiator for project planning meetings, she developed a list of people who were critical to the project at the first stage. It turned out to be about half the number who had previously attended. Those not on the list were simply not invited, and if they showed up anyway (some persisted!) they were politely asked to leave.

The results were immediate. The planning meetings were more highly focused and more was accomplished in less time. When projects moved into implementation stages, Major Fisher invited those who were affected to briefing meetings.

Larger groups work well when the communication is essentially one-way. For example, when a general announcement must be made, and it is important that everyone hears it at the same time from the same person, a large group get-together works fine. Also, celebrations, recognition events, and keynote speeches are effective in large group settings. Even in these settings, it is often a good idea to break the large group into smaller sub-groups for part of the meeting to discuss reactions, generate ideas, and set action steps. If you don't want feedback, the group can be any size.

If your group has more than a dozen members, such as a board, consider running "in-between" meetings with a subset of a larger group. One volunteer board on which I served held executive committee meetings midway between regular monthly meetings to review issues and make decisions that did not require the attention of the full 20-member board. In this case, the limits of the executive committee were clearly spelled out, so that they don't overstep their authority. Also, their actions were communicated via e-mail to all board members. As a result, the regular board meetings were cut from several hours to an average of an hour and a half. Board members now enjoy attending, because the meetings matter.

The Internet enables collaborative meetings that include an unlimited number of participants. A wide range of tools is available for Web-enabled meetings that allow anyone with access to a computer and Internet connection to participate. For example, using a cross-platform program such as GoogleDocs, invited participants can add to an idea-generation thread by simply inserting their comments into a document that is accessible to other invitees. As others add their input, either live or asynchronously, the document grows to include the contributions of all.

Organizations with far-flung locations can stage Webinars that enable others to see and hear the proceedings. The origination point can be someone's desktop or at an elaborately staged studio setting, and the method of delivery can range from an audio teleconference supported by visuals on a Website viewed at individual workstations to simulcast presentations on large screens in theatre-style conference rooms.

CONSIDER HAVING PART-TIME ATTENDEES

It is not always necessary for all participants to attend the entire meeting. One way to do this is to meet with the entire group for items of common interest. After the general issues are covered, anyone except those who are directly affected by the remaining specific items is free to leave.

At a chemical plant in Texas, the 12 engineering department supervisors met every morning for about one hour. Even though one purpose of these meetings was to coordinate crews and schedules, they were not highly structured, nor were they productive. The most frequent agenda item was "who brought the donuts?" Because the group met every day, there was a lot of kidding around and socializing.

Juanita, the manager in charge, estimated the cost of the daily meetings by calculating an hourly equivalent of the salaries and benefits of everyone attending. The result was a meeting cost of $560 per hour. This translated to $2,800 a week for five meetings and more than $140,000 a year, if the meetings averaged an hour in length. And this was just one work group!

Then, she asked participants to guesstimate what they could be doing with their time if they were not involved in the daily meetings. Although this opportunity cost was more difficult to calculate, it was estimated to range from at least as high, up to double the salary cost for time squandered in meetings.

As a result of this analysis, Juanita suggested cutting the meetings to twice a week, and had the entire group attend for only a half-hour. Schedules were sent to participants in advance via e-mail, and coordinated by one of the supervisors, on a rotating basis. The group decided to make these stand-up meetings, and each person was given two to three minutes to cover key issues and answer any questions from others. If any supervisors had problems or specific issues to discuss, those who were involved stayed on. The rest of the business of the group was conducted asynchronously via e-mail and one-on-one meetings. Eventually, the schedules were posted on an intranet site, which all supervisors could access. The combination of the stand-up huddles and electronic posting of status reports has greatly increased the productivity of this department, and the idea has been expanded to other areas of the plant.

If senior executives are pressed for time, suggest that they attend either at the beginning to set the stage, or during the last few minutes of a meeting to review the output of others, ask and answer questions, and approve the recommendations.

Consider Not Attending Meetings of Marginal Interest to You

This bold move may be tricky if your boss is the initiator (person calling the meeting). However, you may be applauded for astutely managing your priorities! One way to approach this is to explain to the initiator what other things are on your to-do list, which you believe are more important than spending time in a meeting of minor relevance to you.

Of course, the initiator may have reasons to invite you that he or she doesn't make clear initially. Your request to skip the meeting may prompt more candid communications about the purpose. Maybe your objective point of view is needed. Sometimes it is productive to have a marketing person view a manufacturing issue or a volunteer coordinator review the budget. Then there's the possibility that the initiator may agree with your assessment, and excuse you from attending.

As the new minister of a Presbyterian church in central Arizona, Pastor Arnie was invited to attend every meeting held by every committee in the church. At first, Arnie thought this was useful, because it gave him a good understanding of what each group did, and it was a good way to get to know some of the more active members.

Through time, Pastor Arnie began to realize the committee chairs wanted more than his attendance. They wanted him to make or "bless" major decisions, which is the way they had functioned with the previous minister. He also sensed that the conversations were somewhat guarded when he was present. Because Arnie preferred to let the committees decide most things on their own, he began to "uninvite" himself from the meetings, and ask that he be kept informed by the chair or the meeting notes.

Initially, the committee chairs thought Arnie did not care, and some resented his absence from their meetings. They realized, however, how much more enthusiastic committee members felt when they were empowered to discuss and decide things on their own. Occasionally, Arnie would be brought into critical discussions on a timely basis, but the committee chairs functioned much more effectively without the pastor being involved in every detail.

Use the meeting as a learning opportunity

If you find yourself "trapped" in a meeting that isn't relevant or important to you, and there is no way out, why not use the occasion to observe the process and learn something? For example, focus on what is happening to make the meeting effective or not—what is the meeting initiator or facilitator doing that makes the meeting work well? Who is participating and who is not? If you are an "outsider," you may find that your detachment from the subject gives you clarity and the ability to contribute useful ideas and suggestions. If you are totally bored, ask the facilitator at the break if you might help by serving as recorder or timekeeper.

Assign Key Roles to Make the Meeting Function Smoothly

In the typical small group meeting, there are only two roles identified: the initiator (often called the leader) and everybody else! Sometimes, a recorder is appointed, often accompanied by groans of "Do I have to?" However, meetings can take quantum leaps in effectiveness if people are assigned key roles and perform the functions of those roles. We identified these roles in the introduction. Here is some more detail about each:

The **initiator** is the person who calls the meeting, clarifies the purpose and expected outcomes, decides who attends, and sets the tone. He or she "owns" the issue or challenge, and is generally responsible for its resolution. The initiator is often the elected or appointed head of a group, such as the manager, chair, committee head, or team leader. With the facilitator, the initiator plans the agenda.

The **facilitator** designs the agenda with the initiator, and is charged with running the meeting process, keeping things on track, and keeping people involved. In most situations, the facilitator is obligated to remain neutral on issues, and focuses on process rather than the content of the meeting. The facilitator serves the group by helping the initiator and participants achieve the purpose and outcomes.

The **recorder** takes notes without editing or evaluating during the meeting and distributes a summary of key discussion points and action/follow-up items afterward. He or she may do this via a notepad, flip chart, electronic white board, or computer.

The **timekeeper** keeps track of time, and notifies the facilitator and group of starting and ending times for discussion topics at appropriate points during the meeting.

Participants are the main players in a meeting. Their job is to prepare properly, share information and ideas, express opinions, analyze issues, and generally contribute to achieving the meeting purpose.

Resource people prepare and present information, answer questions, and contribute advice of a general or specific nature.

It may seem like overkill to have all these roles in a meeting of just a few people. It's not. With these roles clearly identified and performed satisfactorily, your meeting will become more effective. You'll get more things done in less time and keep everyone involved and interested throughout.

For many functions, people may serve in more than one role, such as assigning the timekeeper role to one of the participants. However, there is one major trap to avoid. Most groups get into trouble by combining the roles of initiator and facilitator. Why? The main reason is that the initiator is often the most powerful person in the meeting because of his or her title or authority, and usually has strong points of view on the issues to be discussed. After all, the initiator calls the meeting, which, by itself, carries a level of influence or authority. By contrast, the facilitator is charged with running the meeting process. By definition, the facilitator must be impartial and neutral on issues and ideas.

Some meeting initiators do a good job of facilitating…until an issue comes up in which they have a strong opinion or vested interest. It is very difficult to stay neutral when this happens.

Early in my career, the Mennen Company (now part of Colgate) sent me and five other people to a weeklong facilitator training course. The idea was that we would return to the company, and be available to internal departments to help plan and facilitate meetings. All of us were line managers, and we committed to finding the time to facilitate other groups in the company. We mostly facilitated idea generation and process/product improvement sessions for each other's teams, and the results were extremely positive.

As our facilitation skills were honed, each of us was tempted to facilitate our own sessions, that is, meetings that we also initiated. Almost immediately, we found out that we could not be neutral on issues in which we had a vested interest. As a result, we went back to trading off, so that we could fully participate in our own meetings, and facilitate meetings for each other's teams.

Some leaders (meeting initiators) may be uncomfortable having someone else run "their" meeting. This might be a control issue, or a perception that having a facilitator somehow diminishes their authority. If initiators are trained in facilitation skills—some are—and can remain neutral throughout, then combining the two roles may work.

But even if it does succeed, what's the benefit? Running an effective meeting is hard work, and it precludes initiators from fully participating in the content issues. If you are the boss, you are too valuable to be overly concerned about the techniques and logistics of running an effective meeting. After observing and participating in hundreds of meetings, it is clear to me that it is nearly impossible to be the decision-maker and still run a fair, non-manipulative meeting. Taking the first step to separate the role of the initiator from the role of the facilitator is a big one, but the results are worth it. Initiators who have made this transition report to me that having someone else facilitate actually frees them up to fully participate in discussions.

It is sometimes possible and often practical to combine the roles of facilitator and recorder. The trade-off is that it slows down the meeting process. This important subject will come up again in Chapter 5.

Resource people are sometimes outsiders, but quite often they are group members. For example, the initiator may present some information, and any participant may also be a resource person. As noted, the time-keeper and recorder duties are frequently handled by one or more of the participants.

For best results, meeting roles should be rotated. When several people in a group are trained and prepared to facilitate, group effectiveness usually improves. Most people can learn how to be an effective recorder without too much difficulty. Rotating these responsibilities keeps more people involved, and helps educate members about group process, meeting dynamics, and time management.

The Function of Meeting Planners

Many organizations have full-time or part-time meeting planners, or outsource this function to consulting groups or specialists. Because planners are utilized most often for larger, more complex meetings and events, this book does not address the planning functions as a separate role. If there is no designated meeting planner, the meeting preparation steps usually fall to the initiator or facilitator, or perhaps an administrative assistant.

If your organization is fortunate enough to have the services of a meeting planner, he or she can assist considerably in making sure the planning and logistics are covered thoroughly. Meeting planners are trained to "sweat the small stuff," know the right questions to ask, and how to deal with hotels and conference facilities. To use meeting planners effectively, involve them in the early stages of planning and share as much information with them as possible.

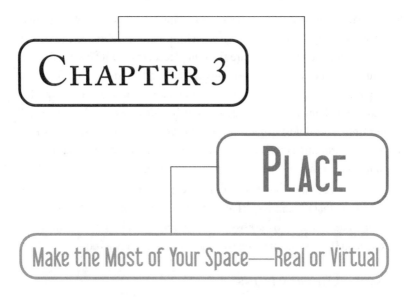

CHAPTER 3

PLACE

Make the Most of Your Space—Real or Virtual

The Truth You Never Hear

"I guess the room we wanted was already taken, so we'll just squeeze in here. I'm sorry there's not enough room for all of you to sit down, so some of you will have to stand. It's a little hot in here, but we've asked them to adjust the thermostat. Geez, that air blower is making a lot of noise, so you may have trouble hearing what's going on…"

The Challenges

ROOM INAPPROPRIATE FOR MEETING

You are in a room that is clearly wrong for the meeting. It would hold a small army, yet there are only eight of you huddled in a lonely corner. The size of the room, along with its dark, massive furnishings, suggests an air of formality that hardly seems conducive for brainstorming new ideas. At the opposite extreme, 15 people are meeting in a room that comfortably holds six. Some people are forced to stand or otherwise deal with their discomfort throughout the meeting.

Most business offices have one or more rooms suitable for small group meetings. However, I have been in many conference rooms that have large, oversized furniture fixed in place. Depending on the size and setup, only a few types of meetings can be conducted comfortably in the room. Churches, schools, hospitals, community centers, and other special-purpose buildings usually have excellent facilities for everything but small meetings. You know what this means if you have ever attended a PTA finance committee meeting in a kindergarten classroom, or a training session in the corner of a gymnasium or dining area.

I suspect many meetings are held without a lot of thought given to the impact that the space will have on the meeting's purpose. For example, it might never occur to the boss that a meeting in her office sets a different tone than if the same meeting were held in a conference room.

NOISE DISTRACTIONS

If you hold a meeting in a hotel or conference facility, you can almost bet there will be distracting noises from the banquet in the adjoining room or clatter emanating from the kitchen. By their very nature, conference and breakout rooms have to be flexible to accommodate a variety of meeting sizes and types, so you will find movable walls in such places. Unfortunately, this often results in sound leaks from one meeting to another, or from the kitchen. Other distractions can come from the loud ambient noise of heating or cooling systems, from workers vacuuming the carpet in the next room, or from lawnmowers just outside your meeting room window. More than once, I have facilitated or attended a meeting accompanied by distracting piped-in music that no one knew how to turn off.

Electronic meetings are not immune, either. The problem of noise may be compounded in meetings where two or more participants are calling in from remote locations. For example, if several people are having a teleconference, chances are that you will hear computer keyboards clicking away, other phones ringing, airport PA announcements, near-by cell phone conversations, or other distracting sounds, depending on the location of participants. The problem is that noise distractions divert the group's attention to the noise source, and some participants will not be able to hear or track the conversation.

ROOM SETUP NOT CONDUCIVE TO MEETING'S PURPOSE

When little thought is given to how chairs and other furnishings are arranged, subtle dynamics come into play that can affect a meeting's effectiveness. For example, in a session designed to generate ideas, a room arrangement that does not allow group members to interact easily with each other will not be as effective as one that does.

Why are the place and space so important? The room sets a tone for the meeting. If it is inviting, people will feel better and are likely to be better participants. If the meeting room is not right, it can drain participants' energy and contribute to a less effective meeting. Whatever the choice for meeting room, there is also the issue of setup—it's almost as if there is an unwritten rule that meetings have to take place with everyone sitting around a table. Often this "rule" can be broken with excellent results.

Two recent meetings I attended dramatize the impact of the meeting space environment on results. The purpose of each meeting was to generate ideas: one for new products and the other for retail merchandising concepts for a line of beverages.

As I walked into the room for the new products session, I could almost feel my energy draining. The room was drab and cluttered with boxes of materials; big overstuffed chairs were set up around a massive conference room table. Because the chairs were so large, there was little room for anyone to move. They weren't that comfortable, either. The lighting was poor, and the walls were bare, except for a faded print that looked half a century old. Although this meeting was held in the 21st century, the setting was definitely a throwback to the mid-1970s.

By contrast, the room used for developing the beverage merchandising concepts was modern, bright, and festive. Participants felt immediately intrigued and energized when they entered the room. Two areas were set up within a larger space—one had movable tables and chairs, and was used for presenting material and for voting to select the best concepts. The second area—where we generated ideas—held sofas and comfortable chairs, colorful decorations, product displays and sketches, subgroup breakout areas, plants, and bright lighting. The marketing agency working on this project spent considerable time and energy creating these spaces, which provided a highly stimulating environment.

Although useful ideas were generated in both sessions, it was an uphill battle in the new products group to overcome the negative room dynamics. There was no question that the environment in the merchandising idea session contributed to high energy and a substantial output of creative ideas from participants.

Strategies and Solutions for Meeting Spaces

⇨ Evaluate size, location, furnishings, lighting, and other dynamics in view of the purpose of the meeting. Select a space that will help participants focus on this purpose, with as few distractions as possible.

⇨ Hold meetings in neutral territory, if possible.

⇨ Arrange the room to help the group accomplish the meeting purpose.

⇨ Have occasional stand-up meetings.

⇨ Hold a meeting outside, or in an unusual space to stimulate thinking. Recognize that informal gatherings will take place outside the regular meeting room.

⇨ Consider holding a virtual meeting.

Place

EVALUATE SIZE, LOCATION, FURNISHINGS, AND OTHER DYNAMICS

There are many factors related to the meeting space that can affect a group's productivity. This list will give you an idea of some of the things you should consider.

Ideal size

The room should be large enough for every participant to be comfortable, and small enough for some degree of intimacy. Twelve people seated in an auditorium would feel overwhelmed by the room; 10 people in a typical office would be cramped. Additional tips:

⇨ If the meeting purpose is to generate ideas, allow enough space for flip charts, computers, or other tools at the front of the room.

⇨ If a presentation is involved, arrange the room so that everyone can easily see the presenter and projected image (if PowerPoint is being used), and there is plenty of space for the presenter(s) to move around.

⇨ If the room is too large, use plants or screens to section off the meeting area. You may also wish to set up breakout areas in the room (or in other rooms) for small group collaboration. Portable chairs make this easier to implement on the fly.

Ideal location

The room should be convenient for all and easy to find. No one likes to be embarrassed by being late to a meeting simply because they couldn't locate the room.

Look for the space that is best suited for your meeting's purpose.

Provide maps and clear directions if there is any doubt about how to locate the room. If you have ever arrived on time or early for a meeting, only to spend several minutes wandering around unfamiliar buildings looking for conference room 4 West A or some other mysterious code, you will appreciate this suggestion. What is familiar to insiders may not be apparent to guests.

Ideal furnishings

Strive for seating that is comfortable, but not too plush; a table or hard surface to write on (except for most theater style arrangements); tables for materials, A/V equipment, and food. Live plants and artwork add warmth to meeting spaces. If there is a window in the room, make sure the view, the glare, or the heat coming through are not distracting.

⇨   If you are in a room with a fixed conference table, arrange the chairs so that everyone is able to see and interact with all participants. If there are more chairs than participants, remove some of the chairs if possible.

⇨   As noted, chairs that are portable can be arranged and rearranged in multiple ways to encourage collaboration in team breakouts. (See more on room arrangements below.)

⇨   For meetings to generate ideas, toys, puzzles, and games inspire playful thinking and open-minded creativity.

Ideal lighting

Bright, indirect lighting is usually best. If the room has dimmers, use them to vary the intensity as needed. For example, you may want to dim the lights a bit if computer visuals are shown. Never, ever turn off all the lights during a meeting! I am always amazed and amused when presenters asked for the room lights to be dimmed or turned off when they fire up their computers for a PowerPoint presentation or video…especially right after lunch. It is an open invitation for participants to doze off and tune out. Most LCD and other projectors are bright enough to leave the room lights at normal levels and still allow everyone to read the computer slides.

Place

Ideal heating and ventilation

Room temperature should be comfortable, with good circulation and the ability to regulate to temperature. The two most frequent complaints I hear from meeting participants is "the room is too warm" and "the room is too cold."

Adjustable heating or cooling is a must. Keep the room on the cooler side (68° to 70°) at first; the effect of body heat will kick in soon enough to make it comfortable for everyone.

If you find yourself in a room with a loud blower from the heating or cooling system, try to change the location of your meeting, or at least have it turned off except during the breaks.

Ideal access

The meeting room should be close to bathrooms and break areas, and provide access for any physically challenged persons attending.

Ideal noise level

Look for low ambient noise, no major distractions, and no surprises. At a planning workshop to create a long-term vision for a company, we had reached an agreement on a vision statement at the end of a long morning session. At the moment the final vision statement was written on a flip chart and signed off by the team, we heard a group singing "God Bless America" in the adjacent room. Normally, having the Rotary Club luncheon meeting in the next room would be distracting, but in this case it was momentous.

Hold the Meeting in Neutral Territory

A meetings held in someone's office usually gives him or her a subtle advantage. If it is the boss's office, it can be intimidating to others. For the best results, select a site for meeting that favors no one person or entity. A conference room is almost always a good choice. Why else do you suppose so many meetings involving world powers are held in neutral countries and locations?

If there is no other choice than to meet in someone's office, try to avoid having the boss sit behind a desk, which places a barrier between him or her and other participants. If there is enough room, set up chairs in a separate area of the office. Fortunately, many larger offices have a separate conference area—use it.

Arrange the Room to Help Accomplish the Purpose

If you want everyone to be involved—and why wouldn't you?—the best way to encourage it is to allow group members to see each others' faces. Assuming you have the option to set up the room to your specifications, consider what is best for your purpose. The configurations that are most advantageous for easy discussions and collaboration are circles, squares, semicircles, and U-shaped seating arrangements. Most other room setups force some people to look at the backs of heads.

Circles and squares

These can be set up with or without a table.

⇨ Advantages: Circles and squares encourage active participation from everyone; it is not easy to hide. Circles "equalize" participants and smaller circles, or "rounds" of six to 10 people allow small group discussion within a larger room.

⇨ Drawbacks: A large circle or square setup can be unwieldy for larger groups. There is also no focal point for presentations or "group notes." If ideas need to be written on flip charts, some members will have to break the circle to see. It is sometimes difficult to use audiovisual equipment effectively. Circles intensify the mood of the group; squares do this also, but to a lesser extent. Because energy is directed at other people, this may be too intense for some meetings. The intensity increases if there is no table—this can be positive or negative, depending on the group.

⇨ When to use circles: for groups of up to 10 to 12, especially for committee reporting, discussion, and group idea-generation; "rounds" of four to 10 people (with or without a table) are a good setup for larger meetings where sub-groups or breakouts will be formed for discussion, feedback, and collaboration. If participants are sitting at round tables, it is easy for some to move their chairs to see a presentation, and then rejoin the circle for a small group discussion at the table.

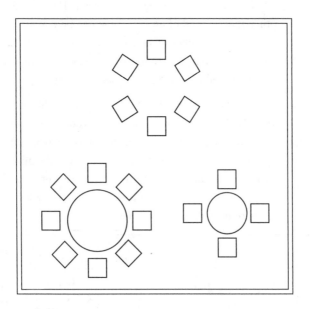

Ovals and rectangles

Oval and rectangular room setups are obviously similar to circles and squares, with some subtle yet important differences; many conference rooms have a semi-permanent oval table in them.

⇨ Advantages: Ovals have most of the same advantages of circles: they are conducive to active participation, because everyone can see most other participants.

⇨ Drawbacks: Participants on the "long" sides sit facing others across the table, which could be intense; yet, they may be unable to see or connect with people sitting to their right or left. I have seen participants in meetings around oval tables "take sides," such as members from the marketing department sitting on one side of the table and operations on the other. Strangely, men and women often sit on opposite sides, as if the meeting were a junior high school dance. By all means, mix people in an oval seating arrangement. The person sitting at either end of an oval table can be perceived as "more equal" than others; not surprisingly, the boss often sits at one end. If you're the boss, you may want to sit around the table rather than at the end.

⇨ When to use ovals: when you don't have a choice. You will find oval tables in conference rooms more often than not. Staff and committee meetings can work effectively in oval configurations, especially if the initiator does not assume the head position at one end. Leave one end of the table open if the meeting includes presentations with A/V equipment.

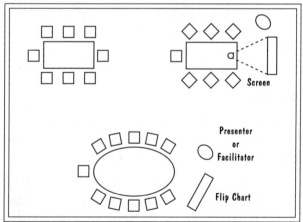

Place

Semicircle and U-shaped

⇨ Advantages: By placing A/V screens, projectors, white boards, and flip chart easels at the open end, semicircles provide a natural focal point on presenters or the facilitator and the work of the group. It's easy to make eye contact and it promotes interactive participation. A semicircle not as intense as a circle or square, and it allows the facilitator or presenters to move in and out of the "U."

⇨ Drawbacks: This seating form can be unwieldy for groups larger than 10 or 12. Using this setup without tables provides intimacy, which is appropriate for some groups, and too intense for others. Sometimes space limitations or fixed furniture in meeting rooms make semicircles or U-shapes impractical.

⇨ When to use semicircles or U-shape: These arrangements work well for presentations, meetings to generate ideas, solve problems, or any meeting where lots of collaboration and interaction is desired.

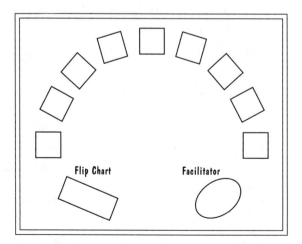

Flip Chart   Facilitator

Theater style

Here chairs are in placed in rows facing front, often without tables.

⇨ Advantages: This is the best configuration to fit the most people in the least amount of space. It focuses on the facilitator, presenters, and visual material at the front of the room.

⇨ Drawbacks: Rooms set up theater-style inhibit intimacy and cohesion among participants. It is difficult to encourage interaction among participants, and is not conducive to "instant" small group breakouts if chairs are fixed. Theater-style room setups place an intense focus on the presenter, which may or may not be desirable. Except for college lecture rooms, this setup does not usually include tables. If participants want to take notes, they have to use their laps, which can be awkward.

⇨ When to use theater style: This setup is appropriate for large group gatherings, especially when information is being delivered one-way, such as speeches and presentations, and little interaction is desired. TIP: angle the chairs in a V-shape if possible, which is somewhat more intimate than straight on.

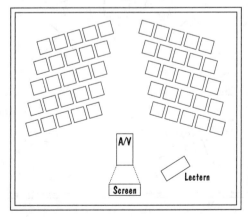

Place

Classroom style

In this setup, chairs are placed with tables facing front—straight or at angles—or desks if the meeting literally takes place in a classroom.

⇨ Advantages: This arrangement accommodates more people per square foot than circles or ovals, although less than theater style; because the setup almost includes tables, it gives participants a surface for writing.

⇨ Drawbacks: It can remind participants of being in school, which isn't always pleasant for some. It minimizes participation, and there is little eye contact or intimacy among participants, unless you angle the chairs and tables.

⇨ When to use classroom style: This works for training situations or one-way presentations, where it is desirable for participants to take notes, and where little audience interaction is called for. Create an angle if possible.

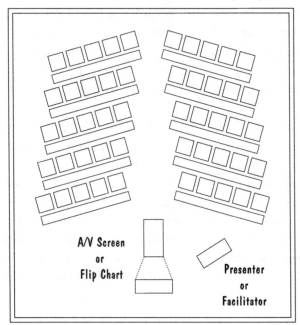

A/V Screen
or
Flip Chart

Presenter
or
Facilitator

Change the Room Setup Often for Long Meetings

For several years, I have facilitated a three-day conference for owners and principals of communications services agencies. The "Sedona Round Table" is attended by 15 to 20 entrepreneurs and executives from around the country. Throughout the course of the three days, participants will find themselves meeting around a U-shaped table, at round tables of six to eight people, or in informal meetings at various corners of the room. Participants may be standing or in chairs. They will meet inside various spaces of the conference hotel, or outside if weather permits. The initiator of the conference, Al Croft, and I have learned that everyone sitting around a table in the same configuration over a multiday conference is tiresome—we have had much better results using multiple setups and spaces.

Stand-up meetings

One of the most effective ways to stay focused and accomplish things in less time is to have a stand-up meeting. To be certain, standing for extended periods can be tiresome, but for quick check-in meetings or idea-generation sessions, standing up keeps the meeting shorter and everyone more alert. Stand-up meetings work best for groups up to 10 people, and with everyone in a circle. In longer meetings, having participants stand up for breakouts or round-robin discussions keeps the energy flowing.

Meetings that occur outside the meeting room

Have you ever attended a meeting in which very little seemed to be happening in the meeting room, yet things were accomplished, usually following a break? These impromptu meetings naturally occur informally. When there is a large group, when participants do not know one another, or when there are diverse issues that are difficult to resolve in a large group, the real discussions and decisions may take place outside the meeting room. This is analogous to the legal maneuver of discussing things at sidebar, in the judge's chambers, or settling matters out of court.

Place

When I worked for Dr Pepper, I attended a meeting at a major motion picture studio that included representatives for a popular rock band, our advertising agency, and the studio. We were scheduled to negotiate a three-way tie-in promotion involving my company's product, a movie soon to be released, and a poster of the artists, who appeared in the movie. Each of the groups brought their entourage of advisors to the meeting; in all, 18 people attended.

The meeting was held in a large conference room, and was characterized by much blustering and posturing. We were going nowhere fast, until we took a break. During the time out, the head studio representative, the artists' manager, and I started chatting informally about what each of us wanted, and what each of us was prepared to contribute to the tie-in promotion. Dr Pepper wanted to associate with the artist and provide an incentive for purchase; the studio wanted publicity for the movie, and the artists wanted to sell records. After considering what each entity could contribute, we reached an agreement in less than five minutes. When the meeting resumed, we announced our decision to the somewhat surprised group, and turned the focus of the meeting from fruitless wrangling to a serious discussion of *how* we were going to make the promotion happen. Since then, I have always been attuned to gatherings and "mini-meetings" that happen informally outside of and around a regular meeting.

Recognizing that important discussions and informal sub-meetings are likely to occur within the context of a larger meeting, why not incorporate them into the agenda? Simply suggest that participants pair off or meet in small sub-groups for an extended break to work things through and bring ideas back to the large meeting. See additional ideas on agendas in Chapter 4.

Virtual meetings

A growing number of meetings take place electronically—either via the Internet, voice or video conference calls, Web-assisted means, or a combination. Most of these types of meetings take place in a number of locations simultaneously, although many are asynchronous virtual meetings, where participants participate on their own schedule. In phone conferences, participants can be anywhere, and if the meeting involves the Internet, most participants will be at a desk or laptop workstation. Chapter 14 covers these types of meetings in detail.

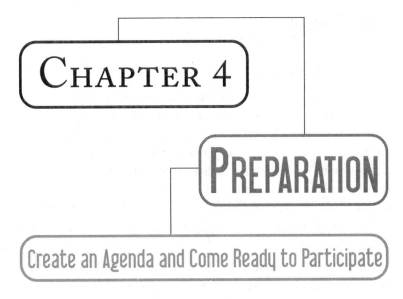

CHAPTER 4

PREPARATION

Create an Agenda and Come Ready to Participate

The Truth You Never Hear

"Because we didn't bother to give you any material to review in advance, we're handing out the 25-page study now, so we can waste everyone's time together. After a few minutes, I'll ask for your comments, which won't count for much, because there's no way you can absorb it all in a short time."

And the Statement You Hear All Too Often

"Oops! My computer screen is frozen. Well, let's see here...does anybody know what key to press to...maybe it's the F-7 Key...oh heck, now the whole thing crashed. Oh well, I can probably wing it without the PowerPoint slides. Let's see—where do we start?"

The Challenges

Participants Are Not Prepared

You are invited to a meeting, but feel uncomfortable because you are not prepared to comment intelligently on the subjects being discussed. Even if you know what the meeting is supposed to be about, you and others may be at a great disadvantage if nothing was given to you in advance to review. Often, the meeting disintegrates into a rambling discussion, and the participants learn that they'll have to review or study for another meeting, when they'll finally address the real topic. The "wheels fall off" many meetings if people are not properly prepared to discuss the issues.

Every Monday morning, the administrative and medical department heads attended a weekly operating meeting at County Memorial Hospital. Ed, the CEO, led these meetings, conducting them in a heavy-handed authoritarian style. The agenda, if there was one, was seldom announced in advance, so none of the participants knew what or how to prepare. As a result, they were clueless, and could only guess at the items on the CEO's radar screen. Invariably, Ed would ask them to comment or report on subjects they weren't prepared to intelligently discuss.

These debilitating meetings covered whatever topics Ed felt like discussing, and often veered off in many directions. The department heads were frequently embarrassed in front of their peers, and their only consolation was that no one was spared; eventually everyone had their "turn in the barrel." Given Ed's style, there was no way the staffers could prepare for these weekly meetings.

Another wasteful practice is to spend time reading through material that could have been distributed in advance. Instead of using the face-to-face meeting to discuss reactions or to discuss issues and collaborate, much time is spent in simply absorbing material for the first time. Humans read and comprehend at different speeds, so some will finish early, while others will struggle to finish, regardless of how much time is allowed.

Preparation

Useless Agendas

The process of preparing an effective agenda is often overlooked as a critical step in running a meeting that matters. Many people assume that simply listing subject titles on a piece of paper is all that is necessary. Agendas that are useless share one or more of these characteristics:

⇨ No relationship to the meeting purpose or outcomes.

⇨ Vague or misleading topics.

⇨ Topics are not prioritized or time-bound.

⇨ No indication of how items will be handled.

⇨ No "breathing room" or flexibility in the schedule.

Without an effective agenda, issues of lesser importance often consume most or all of the time in the meeting, and the most important issues frequently are not given the attention they deserve. Often, they have to be postponed until another meeting.

The monthly board meetings of a community theater group were an exercise in futility. The president prepared an agenda based on whatever details she thought needed the board's attention. Two standard agenda items were old business and new business. Generally, these catchall categories were an open invitation to discuss virtually anything. One evening the board spent more than two hours discussing ad nauseum a "new business" item: whether or not to raise the price charged for intermission refreshments. Of course, there were many excursions (such as the pros and cons of Sprite vs. 7-Up) that were not really all that important. At that same meeting, the board members spent less than 10 minutes discussing how to increase their contributor base, which was a far more important topic.

Many meeting initiators and participants need a dose of reality when it comes to estimating the time required to fully discuss and develop issues. Invariably, they misjudge and underestimate, often by a long shot.

Lack of Ground Rules

Another frequently overlooked area is to determine the ground rules for how a meeting will be conducted. Ground rules are process-related agreements that generally apply throughout the meeting. Most ground rules cover group behavior, such as allowing only one person to talk at a time. Without deciding in advance how things will be done, much is left to chance, and the meeting can slip downhill fast. In the absence of ground rules, the initiator or facilitator might invent arbitrary rules on the spot, which can result in chaos and resentment by participants.

It is easy for meetings to bog down when there are no established ground rules for how items will be introduced, how subjects will be discussed, what happens when a discussion drifts off-topic, how ideas will be collected and evaluated, how decisions will be made, and how disruptive behavior will be handled. Among the more confusing meeting rules, often in nonprofit board meetings, are vague references to Robert's Rules of Order or parliamentary procedure, especially when the person quoting them doesn't have a clue as to what the rules are and how they might be utilized.

Logistics Not Covered

A final area of preparation involves logistics. If you have attended meetings where the computer or projector crashes, the handouts aren't ready, the room is way too hot, or the coffee doesn't show up, you've witnessed how the smallest details can derail a meeting. At their worst, they can effectively shut down a meeting.

At a pivotal meeting with a client, Andrew was poised to recommend a training program for their field service personnel. Or so he thought. He had prepared PowerPoint slides to support the proposal, and planned on using his laptop and portable LCD projector. The day before the meeting, his client suggested that Andrew just burn his presentation slides to a CD, and then run it on their computer and conference room projector. That sounded like a reasonable solution, and something that Andrew often did as a backup, so he transferred the presentation to a CD.

Preparation

On the day of the presentation, Andrew arrived an hour early just to be safe, compact disc in hand. It was then he learned that the client's network had gone down. The technician said, "No problem…we ought to have it up again in a few minutes." Thirty minutes later, the system was still down, as his client contacts entered the room for the meeting. Andrew had brought along his laptop, but left his portable LCD projector in his office. As the clients settled into their chairs, the conference room projector was flashing all kinds of weird computer messages. The only thing more interesting was the color draining from his face. Andrew's only choices were to reschedule the meeting or invite the eight participants to crowd around his laptop screen. Although the client appeared to understand, the meeting was an unmitigated disaster from Andrew's point of view. Ever since then, Andrew always travels with his laptop *and* his own LCD projector. He also brings a CD or flash drive copy of the presentation for a backup, just in case, and has begun posting his presentation slides to a Website for downloading, if necessary. Andrew has learned there is no such thing as being over-prepared for meeting logistics.

The outcome of many meetings is directly proportional to the amount of forethought and preparation that precedes them. Of course, the things we have already covered—clarifying the purpose, identifying expected outcomes, inviting the right people, and selecting and arranging the meeting space—are all essential preparation steps. This chapter will cover several others.

Strategies and Solutions for Effective Preparation

⇨ Everyone attending should prepare for the meeting.

⇨ Draw up a purpose-driven agenda.

⇨ Determine effective ground rules.

⇨ Make a checklist for logistics arrangements.

EACH PERSON ATTENDING SHOULD PREPARE FOR THE MEETING

What should the initiator do before the meeting?

⇨ Establish the purpose of the meeting and decide if the meeting is truly necessary.

⇨ Determine who will attend, including part-time attendees. Coordinate schedules if necessary.

⇨ Decide how much participation (feedback, discussion, and so on) is desired, and how decisions will be made in the meeting.

⇨ Appoint a facilitator and recorder. Work with the facilitator to define outcomes, determine the agenda, and ground rules.

⇨ Set the place, time, and dress code.

⇨ Invite resource people and let them know specifically what you want them to do in the meeting.

⇨ Prepare or assign materials for participants to review prior to the meeting.

⇨ Send out the meeting invitation, providing as much information as possible, including the purpose, outcomes, agenda, and advance review materials.

What should the facilitator do before the meeting?

⇨ Work with the initiator to clarify the purpose, define the expected outcomes, and develop the agenda.

⇨ Develop a preliminary list of ground rules—see more on ground rules later in this chapter.

⇨ Plan and prepare for logistics, such as room layout, refreshments, breakout areas, audiovisual equipment,

Preparation

and in-room beverages and food. If a meeting planner is assigned, work with him or her to coordinate the details.

⇨ Develop the optimum processes for accomplishing the meeting purpose and working through the agenda. Examples: large group discussion, small group breakouts, presentation with Q&A, exercises, and so on.

What should the recorder do before the meeting?

⇨ Review the notes and action items from the previous meeting, if applicable.

⇨ Decide how notes will be taken and displayed during the meeting, and make sure all materials are available, such as easels, pads, markers, a white board, or a laptop computer.

What should participants do before the meeting?

⇨ Reply to the meeting notice if requested, and block the meeting time. If the meeting is in a remote location, make travel arrangements.

⇨ Give input for the agenda to the initiator or facilitator, if requested.

⇨ Read any relevant materials to prepare for the meeting. Prepare a point of view on key issues.

What should resource people do before the meeting?

⇨ Understand fully the purpose of the meeting and how their expertise can help accomplish it.

⇨ Do research and reading necessary to prepare for the meeting. Prepare materials for participants to review in advance.

⇨   Prepare a presentation for the group, if it's appropriate. Notify the facilitator or meeting planner if A/V equipment is required.

⇨   Check out all audiovisual equipment prior to the meeting.

Prior to idea-generation sessions for new products, I often ask participants to go "shopping" to observe what is happening in their related fields. They are encouraged to make notes, take pictures, or even buy things that interest them. With this kind of involvement, participants are eager to share their observations with the group and use their experiences as springboards for ideas. The night before one session, for example, our group of eight descended upon a supermarket in a strip mall. With the store manager's permission, we brought along a few digital cameras to take pictures. Although our task was to generate ideas for new household cleaning products, everyone was encouraged to visit all parts of the store. We also went to a hardware store and a fast-food restaurant, to see if anything caught our attention. The photos were downloaded into a computer to share with everyone, and we used the visual ideas as springboards for different areas of exploration during the session.

When possible, send advance reading materials via e-mail, post them on a Website or send them by e-mail prior to the meeting, and ask participants to come prepared to discuss their reactions to the material. Never do anything face-to-face that can people can do "off line" at their own pace.

Draw Up a Purpose-Driven Agenda

A well-prepared meeting agenda is like a road map, providing a guide for making the best use of everyone's time, and achieving the purpose. A purpose-driven agenda is a critical step in running meetings that matter.

The initiator and facilitator should work together to prepare a dynamic agenda. The starting point is a clear purpose that defines why the meeting is being held, followed by specific outcomes to be achieved. If either of these is unclear, they should refine them to make them as unambiguous as possible. (See Chapter 1 for guidance in crafting workable purpose and outcome statements.)

Preparation

Each agenda item should help achieve the purpose and outcomes. For example, in a problem-solving session, the purpose might be to generate ideas that increase the throughput of a production line, with a goal (outcome) of developing two alternatives to test. The agenda might include a 10-minute briefing to recap key elements of the problem, a five-minute exercise to loosen up the group's thinking, a 20-minute facilitated discussion to develop speculative possibilities, small group breakouts for 25 minutes to build out ideas and a 15-minute selection process to discuss and select the two ideas for testing. This portion of the agenda might look similar to this:

10:00–10:10	Recap problem	Alex present summary
10:10–10:15	Exercise	Janie facilitate—large group
10:15–10:35	Generate speculations around the problem as stated	Janie facilitate—large group
10:35–11:00	Build ideas and create new possibilities	Small groups—leaders to be appointed
11:00–11:15	Select top two winners against criteria	Sandy review criteria, Janie facilitate

The agenda for a meeting to provide project updates might include a round robin, in which each participant has three to five minutes to let the group know what he or she is working on, what additional resources are needed, or what assistance they can provide to others. Even as you are developing agendas, always look for alternative ways to achieve the purpose without a face-to-face meeting. For example, if project updates can be sent via e-mail or posted on a Website, there may be no need to gather the team together.

Not all agenda items have to be detailed to the nth degree. However, even with a free-flowing discussion, there should be time parameters. For example, if the purpose is to review the current vacation policy, the agenda might include a 20-minute open discussion of the pros and cons of the current policies.

Stay away from agenda items that are vague or open-ended, such as old (or new) business, president's remarks, or business review. If there are unfinished items from previous meetings, they should be listed specifically list, with an indication of what is to be done (discuss, decide, and so on) and how much time it will take. If the president has remarks for the group, list them specifically.

Strive to state agenda items as imperatives, or goals to be achieved; use verbs where possible—they suggest an action or process rather than a static topic. In the previous example, note how most agenda items include verbs, such as recap, speculate, generate, and select.

If you are dependent on others for agenda items—as is often the case in team, committee, or staff meetings—ask participants in advance for the issues they wish to discuss in the group, assigning a priority to each and estimating how much time they require. This advance poll can be done by e-mail, phone, fax, or memo, and it saves time at the meeting. It also prompts participants to consider how they wish to use the group's time on their behalf, and encourages people to come prepared.

Whenever a fuzzy agenda is submitted, such as "Project Red," press for specifics. Will the discussion focus on introducing the project, reviewing it, deciding the budget for it, or summarizing the results?

Once preliminary agenda items and the process for handling them have been identified, estimate the time required for each item. The final step is to list them in order of importance. The agenda is then prioritized, with the most important items first, and so on in descending order of importance. The last items on the agenda should be a few minutes for open items, or "parking lot" items, which we will discuss later, followed by a summary of action items.

When you add up all the agenda items, and the times fall within the total time allocated for the meeting, you have an agenda! If the cumulative agenda items would make you run over, decide if you want to extend the time for the meeting, trim time off of one or more of the agenda items, or eliminate some items.

Preparation

Here is a sample agenda:

Group:	Research Department Staff Meeting
Meeting Date:	December 10
Purpose of meeting:	Generate input for new office layout; update on key projects
Outcomes:	Agree on "musts" and "wants" for layout; agree on work schedules for June

Initiator: G.B. **Facilitator:** Marcia
Recorder: Alan **Timekeeper:** Florence
Attendees: Above, plus Richard, Abby, Jenn, and Rachel

Time	Topics/Process	Discussion Leader
9:00–9:30	Idea generation: How to utilize the new space most effectively. Free-flow discussion for 10 minutes; facilitated idea generation for 20 minutes. Goal: wish list for musts and wants.	G.B. + Marcia
9:30–9:40	Sort out and prioritize ideas.	Marcia facilitate
9:40–10:00	Straw vote for consensus, translate ideas into management presentation.	Group
10:00–10:16	Two-minute updates on key projects.	Gary
10:16–10:26	Parking lot items, announcements.	Linda
10:26–10:30	Recap of action items.	Alan

See the appendix for more sample agendas.

Establish Ground Rules

Ground rules are guidelines that members agree to live by during meetings to make the process run smoothly. Many groups have unspoken ground rules for meetings, which are, through trial and error, understood by all participants throughout time. In other groups, ground rules may be unclear, or subject to change randomly. By examining how you "do" meetings, however, and making the ground rules clear, your meetings can run more smoothly and efficiently.

Although the initiator or facilitator (or both) might be chosen to draw up a list of ground rules, every member of the group must agree to live with them and support them.

For groups that meet regularly, the ground rules should be set once, and then reviewed occasionally—every few months or so—or when the need arises. For ad hoc or newly forming groups, one of the first priorities should be to establish the ground rules by which the group will operate.

Here are some ground rules from different groups that you may want to consider adopting for your meetings:

➪ Meetings will start and end on time, unless group agrees to extend. Anyone absent agrees to support group's decision.

➪ There is only one meeting; no side conversations—only one person may talk at a time.

➪ All viewpoints are valid; no one will be criticized for expressing an opinion.

➪ During brainstorming, ideas will be generated and collected first, evaluated later (see Chapter 7).

➪ The facilitator is in charge of the meeting process; the role of facilitator will be rotated each meeting.

➪ Decisions will be made by modified consensus whenever possible. Voting is a last resort (see Chapter 9). All members will support decisions made by the group.

⇨ All group members will learn and practice constructive meeting skills (see Chapter 6).

⇨ All cell phones, PDAs, BlackBerries, computers, and pagers will be turned off. Check messages only at breaks.

⇨ Presenters and resource people will prepare advance review materials whenever possible. Group members will review materials (or complete assignments) prior to meetings.

To get started, review the ground rules already in effect, even the ones that haven't been officially adopted. Examine these conventions to confirm how they are actually useful, and that everyone is comfortable with them. If you want to make changes, try out a few new ground rules to see if they make things run more smoothly. After you have experimented with new rules, confirm them, and introduce others when the group is ready. Finally, give a copy of the ground rules to everyone involved, or post them in the meeting room.

What happens if ground rules are broken? First, keep in mind that ground rules are intended to help the group accomplish its goals and to conduct more effective meetings. When someone "breaks" a ground rule, the facilitator or any other participant can simply point out what is going on; for example: "hey folks, all ideas are valid—let's hear what Maryanne has to say." Some groups have established consequences for people who violate the agreed-upon ground rules for meetings. One of my business round table groups collects a $5 fine from anyone who is late, or whose cell phones goes off during meetings. The money collected is designated for a specific purpose, such as donating it to a charity or buying snacks for the next meeting. See Chapters 5, 6, and 13 for more ideas enforcing ground rules and controlling behaviors that disrupt meetings.

MAKE A CHECKLIST FOR LOGISTICS PLANNING

The final area to cover in planning for meetings is logistics. This is an area in which people often assume that someone else is handling things. It is easy to be lulled into complacency, especially if you have experienced a streak of good luck when several meetings have already run smoothly. My experience has been that a well-executed meeting does not happen because of good luck, but through careful preparation and attention to logistics matters.

Besides selecting the appropriate room and arranging the furniture to fit the meeting's purpose, there are dozens of other details that need the attention of initiators and facilitators. Your checklist might include:

⇨   Arrange for and check out all audiovisual equipment.

⇨   Be very specific about whether you will need an LCD projector, computer (Mac or PC), hookup cables, Internet access, sound amplification, or other electronic support. If you are using computer-projected visuals, it's usually a good idea to bring a backup CD of presentations, as well as printed copies to use as a last resort.

⇨   Check out all equipment on-site as soon as you arrive, and again just before the meeting.

⇨   Build a meeting "kit." Your kit might include:

➡   Extension cords and power strips.

➡   Flip charts (I am partial to the kind with an adhesive strip on the back) and easels.

➡   Markers for flip charts—the "non-lethal" kind that smell good and don't bleed through.

➡   Pads and pencils or pens for all participants, unless you ask them to bring their own.

➡   Name tags or name tents—these are useful even in an ongoing group if there are new people attending or a guest speaker.

➡   Duct tape or electrical tape to secure wires that someone might trip over.

Preparation

➡️ Materials for exercises, as appropriate.

➡️ A stopwatch, or watch with a second hand, for the timekeeper.

Be sure all written materials, such as handouts, workbooks, and other leave-behinds are prepared and delivered to the meeting room beforehand.

⇨ Materials that are going to be distributed to participants should be prepared well in advance and brought personally to the meeting site by the presenter, facilitator, initiator, or planner.

⇨ If you have handouts for a meeting in an out-of-town location that are too bulky for you to hand carry, send them ahead. One trainer I know sends half of his materials via FedEx and the other half via UPS. If one of them doesn't deliver on time, at least some materials will be available for sharing. Several firms, such as FedExKinko's, allow you to upload electronic files, which will be printed out and waiting for you at your destination. Bring a master of your material just to be safe.

Arrange for breaks and refreshments. Successful meetings longer than two hours include specific times for participants to relax and re-charge. Maslow was right: basic human needs that are unsatisfied take precedence over everything else. It is difficult to think creatively or focus on critical issues if you have to go to the bathroom, or when you are hungry or sleepy. This may seem like a profound statement of the obvious, yet I am amazed at the number of meetings that go on and on with no end in sight, and no relief for the weary.

⇨ If breaks are not planned, what often happens is that people simply take breaks on their own, or tune out mentally, which is just as disruptive. The antidote is to plan frequent breaks as part of the agenda, about every hour—or no more than every 90 minutes.

⇨ A break does not have to be a 20-minute dispersion of the group, which can easily turn into a half hour; after intense "mental work," a three- to five-minute stand-up break in the meeting room or a step outside for fresh air is often just what everyone needs.

⇨ Refreshments are usually included with breaks and may also be available to participants during the meeting. Food is an effective incentive to get people to attend meetings.

⇨ Water should be available at all times in the meeting room, with other beverages as desired, such as coffee, tea, juices, and soft drinks.

⇨ Light snacks may be made available throughout, or only during breaks. Be careful of plying meeting participants with too much sugar or high-fat snacks. They tend to produce a fleeting high, followed by lethargy. Fresh fruit, water, juices, nuts, pretzels, cheese, and cut vegetables are nice alternatives.

Handle visual and sound issues. Well before meeting participants arrive, designate someone to "walk the room," observing anything that might distract people from fully participating in the meeting. Look and listen for things such as:

⇨ Lines of vision that are blocked (change the room arrangement if possible).

⇨ A loud heater blower or ventilation system that makes it difficult to hear one another (turn it off during the meeting, or change rooms if possible).

⇨ Beautiful yet distracting views outside the window (pull the curtains for part of the meeting; open them at the break).

By "pre-experiencing" your meeting, you will become aware of things that support the meeting purpose and things that do not.

Recap of Part I

Before moving on, keep in mind that an ounce of planning is worth a ton of excuses. Remember the four Ps of planning:

1. ***Purpose:*** Be clear about why you are meeting, and link it to outcomes.

2. ***People:*** Make sure the right participants attend, even if some attend part-time.

3. ***Place:*** Choose the right space and set it up to serve your purpose.

4. ***Preparation:*** Construct a purpose-driven agenda, make sure people come prepared, set ground rules, and plan for logistics.

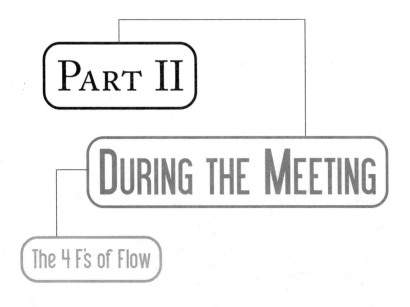

PART II

DURING THE MEETING

The 4 F's of Flow

Focus

Reconfirm purpose, outcomes, and agenda; work the agenda to stay on track; use a timekeeper to be aware of time; record ideas, decisions, and action items.

Facilitation

Encourage all participants to learn and use effective facilitation skills. Empower the facilitator to run the meeting process.

Feedback

Observe and respond to ongoing feedback during the meeting. Always separate generating ideas from evaluating ideas. Learn how to sort and prioritize ideas, then use a balanced response technique to give feedback and turn ideas into solutions.

Fun and Fellowship

Use appropriate humor to lighten things up while getting serious work done; get to know each other as people.

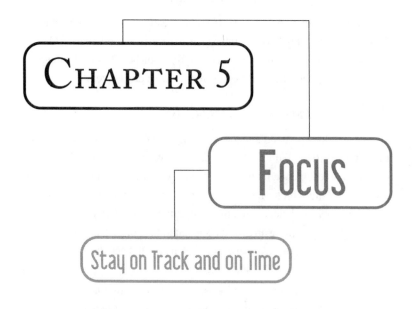

CHAPTER 5

FOCUS

Stay on Track and on Time

The Truth You Never Hear

"Following our usual pattern, our meeting today will probably get off-track after the first few minutes, and we'll probably ramble on for several hours until it's completely out of control, and everyone is completely drained."

The Challenges

GROUP MEMBERS NOT ON BOARD

In many meetings, it is safe to assume that not all members share the same level of interest, understanding, and enthusiasm for the purpose or agenda items. For any number of reasons, people often come to a meeting with other priorities or even personal issues that can influence or over-whelm their participation.

For any single issue or discussion item, some group members will know more about it than others, and everyone will view it through his or her own experience and filters. If some means by which to establish a common starting point is not introduced, there is a good chance that the discussion will ramble and drift until everyone is on board. Body language—especially puzzled or bored expressions—are a dead giveaway.

AGENDA ITEMS NOT MANAGED

Even with a planned agenda, meetings can quickly lose their focus if the group drifts off into other directions. We've already noted that a purpose-driven agenda includes identifying all the relevant issues for the group, deciding which ones are most important, estimating the time required for each, and placing the most important items ahead of less critical items. Simply designing an agenda is no guarantee of a tightly run, smooth flowing meeting. A piece of paper will not, by itself, keep the discussion on track or control disruptive behavior.

When meetings lose their focus, I've observed that most people do not speak up to alert other group members about what is happening. For example, if time runs out before all agenda items are covered, the meeting often just keeps on going, and going...

The discussion can be moving along smoothly, and all of a sudden something happens to throw the meeting out of focus. Perhaps someone interjects a tangent or wanders off on a lengthy "war story," and the discussion leapfrogs to a completely different direction. Sometimes, the group never gets back to the real agenda.

The weekly operating committee meetings of Smithson Food Company were exasperating to most who attended. They were held on Monday mornings, and it seemed to take forever for the group to focus on what was important. Instead, the ops committee members talked about anything that happened to pop up. Some issues were handled in a minute or two, while others took much longer. Policy matters were mingled with operating issues. Eventually, the group began to prepare agendas for the meetings. What they soon discovered was that making an agenda was only part of the solution.

Focus

In a typical meeting, Doug, the always-efficient assistant to the president, would barge in and say something such as, "Are you aware that a truckload of product had to be diverted in Chicago due to the Teamsters' strike? We may miss the promotion date." For the next two hours or so, the operating committee would then focus on solving this crisis, forgetting whatever else might be on the meeting agenda.

Of course, the issues that Doug brought up were important, and it was true that most of the committee members would not have been aware of the crisis situation. It turned out that Doug received calls from different field sales managers every Monday morning, minutes before the weekly meeting. As a result, the topics were not included in the agenda, which was usually prepared the previous Friday. Doug felt it was his responsibility to bring the calamity of the week to the committee's attention.

Similar scenarios were played out almost every Monday, and none of the committee members ever stopped to question whether dealing with the crisis *du jour* was the best use of their time, whether other items might have a higher priority, or even if it was appropriate for the operating committee to deal with the issue. It is no wonder they were all frustrated with the meetings…everybody except Doug, that is!

GROUP'S OUTPUT IS NOT RECORDED

It is easy for meetings to lose focus when important ideas, decisions, and action steps are not captured when they come up. Group members can easily forget about what has been discussed, and the meeting may become repetitive or get bogged down. If they are not recorded, good ideas, potential solutions, decisions, and action steps can "fall off the table," never to reappear. Even if there is someone taking notes, group members may not know what is being captured or lost until the minutes come out, sometimes days later. By then, it may be too late to recapture important discussions or decisions.

Group Energy Is Low

You've been there. After a couple of hours of batting around ideas or analyzing an issue, you feel drained. The few people still involved in the discussion do not seem to notice that you and several others have tuned out. You begin to wonder if you are the only one who is fatigued. *Doesn't anyone else have to go to the bathroom?* When energy is low, group members easily lose their focus, and little is accomplished.

Ideas and Solutions for Staying Focused

⇨ Establish a common starting point at the beginning of the meeting.

⇨ Work the agenda—manage time for individual topics.

⇨ Intervene when necessary to stay on track, and dump wandering discussions in a "parking lot."

⇨ Track the meeting using a "group memory," recording (at a minimum) all decisions and action steps.

⇨ Plan frequent breaks and energizers.

⇨ Stay focused as a participant by being prepared and through active listening and involvement.

Establish a Common Starting Point at the Beginning of the Meeting

It is the job of the initiator or facilitator to remind all participants of the purpose of the meeting, the expected outcomes, why each participant has been invited, and to preview the agenda and time contract. By doing this at the beginning of the meeting, it sets the stage and helps ensure that everyone is starting at the same place. If advance materials have been distributed, it may be appropriate to briefly recap highlights. If group members have different levels of expertise and understanding, one of the initial agenda items might be a summary presentation on key information to level the playing field. If participants have prepared in advance, a useful exercise is to have everyone, in turn, give a one- or two-minute recap of their understanding of the issue(s) on the agenda.

WORK THE AGENDA—MANAGE TIME FOR TOPICS AND OVERALL

A prioritized agenda with estimated time blocks is the major tool to maintain focus in a meeting. Earlier, we used the analogy of the agenda as a road map—to be useful, the facilitator and others need to check the agenda frequently to insure the meeting stays on course and focused.

Preparing accurate time estimates is a learning process. As noted in the previous chapter, it is likely that your estimates for some topics, at first, will give more than enough time for the group to dig into the issues, discuss options, voice concerns, and create solutions. For others, the allocated time won't be nearly enough to do justice to the issue. In my business round table groups, anyone bringing an issue to the group is asked how much time he or she wants for the discussion. After realizing that nearly everyone underestimated the time required to analyze and solve their issues, we began to routinely add 50 percent or so to the estimates, which turned out to be more accurate. As your group gets more experience with how much time discussion items require, your agendas will become more focused and more useful.

If you find yourself in a meeting where an agenda has not been developed in advance, don't worry—just make it the first order of business. This is a good process for staff meetings, project/team meetings, and others that meet regularly. The initiator or facilitator asks everyone for his or her top priority item and time requested. A second go-around gets the second priority issues, and a third time gathers the rest, as time allows.

Post the agenda on a flip chart sheet, send it out to everyone in advance, and have spare copies in the meeting. At the beginning of the meeting, the facilitator should ask if there are any additional items. If so, assign a priority and time estimate, and add them to the list. It is wise to check with group members before preempting a stated agenda item with a new one.

When the meeting gets underway, start with the first item and complete each one before moving to the next, with the timekeeper tracking the time, and reminding members when time is almost up on each item.

As you run through items on the agenda, the timekeeper reminds the group of the total time elapsed and how much remains. Well before it runs out, the group should decide whether to table additional items for a later time, assign them to others to process separately, or extend the length of the meeting. Most people are reluctant to extend meeting times, which is why you make a prioritized agenda—the most important items always get covered first.

The timekeeper should make a note of when specific agenda items begin and end. If discussions run fairly close to the allotted time, that is all that is required—there is no sense quibbling over a minute or two. However, when the estimated time is almost up on an issue that is clearly not completely developed, the timekeeper should let the group know. It is up to the group, with the help of the facilitator, to decide whether to keep discussing the issue or move on. For example, the group may want to work through the rest of the agenda and then revisit the extended issue at the end of the meeting. In some groups, the initiator may make this decision. If it is important enough, a separate meeting may be called to discuss it in more detail, which would also give people time to prepare better for meaningful discussions.

The timekeeper should refrain from making judgments—he or she is not the facilitator; the job is simply to serve the group by monitoring and informing others of the time.

The timekeeper may also alert the facilitator and group members of break times and overall meeting time; for example, "As a reminder, we have 10 minutes left before we break." Time reminders may also be silent—for example, simply raising one's hand, or holding up a card. In Toastmasters, a green/yellow/red light or sign system is used to notify speakers of elapsed and remaining time. Other timekeepers use discreet bells or chimes to remind the group, or simply raise their hand.

When the timekeeper reminds the group that time is up for an item, the facilitator asks group members (or the initiator) if they want to continue on, or bring that issue to a close. If more time is needed, be specific; for example, "We need 15 more minutes on this." In doing so, the group is also agreeing to spend less time on subsequent items, drop some agenda items, or extend the overall time of the meeting.

One way to stay focused when asking for opinions or reactions from everyone is to limit the time—say, one or two minutes each—to go around the table for comments from participants. This will encourage everyone to be concise and stay on the subject.

Be sure to save the last few minutes to cover "parking lot items" (see below), and to recap decisions and action steps.

Intervene When Necessary and Dump Wandering Discussions in a "Parking Lot"

It is normal for most meetings to veer off course at some point; after all, we are human, and most small group meetings are a dynamic and unrehearsed process. Before the meeting is allowed to disintegrate, however, someone must intervene and call for a mid-course correction. Although that "someone" is usually the facilitator, any group member can intervene.

If someone brings up a new subject or something that isn't on the agenda, try the "parking lot" technique. Start a flip chart page with the title "Parking Lot." Whenever an item is brought up that is off the subject, acknowledge it, and suggest that it go into the parking lot; then post it on the sheet. At the end of the meeting, allow time to address parking lot items, even if the action is to defer them until later.

When the discussion strays from the topic being discussed, the facilitator or any other group member may bring this fact to the group's attention. The group can then decide to keep discussing the side issue, or put it in the parking lot and return to the topic. The key is awareness;

knowing how the group is spending its time and why. For example, "Hey folks, we were talking about short-term sales, and somehow we got onto sales training issues. Let's put that in the parking lot and decide how to deal with it later."

TRACK THE MEETING USING A GROUP MEMORY

Many people incorrectly assume that the role of the recorder is similar to a court reporter—transcribing everything that is said in a meeting word for word. This could be the main reason that some people never volunteer for the job! Capturing everything verbatim would be very difficult without stenography skills or a tape recorder to use for transcribing. Unfortunately, most group members do not know if the information captured is accurate until long after the meeting is over, when they receive a copy of the write-up, often called the minutes. If you have ever waded through a verbatim transcript of any meeting, you may find yourself getting lost in the details and missing the main points.

It is far more productive and useful to group members when the recorder captures and displays ideas, decisions, agreements, and action steps as they are discussed. The "group memory" concept is the way to make this happen. The group memory consists of headlines and summary points (or even drawings) written on a flip chart, computer, or white board. Everyone is able to see the meeting output as it happens, and to confirm the accuracy of information. In electronic meetings, the group memory is often displayed on each participant's personal computer, or on a larger screen. With flip charts, the recorder numbers the sheets and hangs them on the wall for quick reference as the meeting progresses. Tip: Change colors of markers between bullet points; this makes the group notes more readable and fun.

The most important skills for a recorder are the ability to listen and summarize accurately without evaluating. The group memory reminds participants of what has already been covered, which minimizes repetition. For example, if someone revisits an issue already covered, the facilitator can simply refer to the group notes and say something such as, "Ed, we've already covered this in some detail. Do you have any new insights to add?"

Recorders also must be able to write or type fast and legibly. Being able to draw simple graphics is a plus. Being able to spell can be useful, but more important is to not be afraid of making spelling mistakes as you go—they can always be corrected later.

The recorder should not be reluctant to ask group members for help to clarify items, or if he or she gets behind in recording. Ultimately, group members are responsible for ensuring the group notes accurately reflect ideas, decisions, and action steps.

White boards or electronic easels may also be used for the group notes. Some products transfer the writing straight to a computer or copier, which generates letter-size pages that may be e-mailed or duplicated and distributed. Other devices shrink regular flip chart pages into letter size pages, which can be copied and distributed to members. In Chapter 10, we'll discuss how the group memory forms the basis for a follow-up meeting summary with action steps.

Plan Frequent Breaks and Energizers

Most people need some kind of break every so often to maintain their focus in a meeting. Let's face it; some of us have shorter attention spans—and smaller bladders—than others! Breaks and energizers help participants to recharge, and provide an opportunity to refocus the meeting. Here are some suggestions for breaks and energizers to keep your meeting focused and flowing:

> ⇨ Try to change something about every 20 minutes. This can be as simple as changing the subject, or the methods of participation. For example, you can introduce a round robin exercise to get everyone's viewpoint on a subject that has been monopolized by a few people.

⇨ Ask presenters to break their material into "bite-size" segments of 20 to 30 minutes with time for questions or discussion after each segment. This provides another opportunity for everyone to absorb the discussion, quickly recap what has been covered, and focus on what is coming up.

⇨ Have a ground rule that allows any member to call a mini-break any time he or she senses the group is dragging or has low energy. After a break, remember to refocus on the subject, perhaps by a quick recap of what has happened so far, recalibrating the remaining time and setting up the remaining agenda items.

⇨ Plan a formal break every hour or hour and a half. Most breaks will last around 15 to 20 minutes, which will allow enough time for most people to stretch, grab refreshments, and go to the bathroom. It is likely that many people will also check e-mail or voice-mail messages during breaks. Inevitably, some will get involved returning cell phone calls or responding to e-mails. Although this is not encouraged, make sure participants step out of the meeting room, so others won't be disturbed. Most importantly, do not reward them by delaying the restart of the meeting.

⇨ Energizers and games are widely used by trainers and many facilitators, and can enhance and refocus any meeting. For example, a brainteaser or puzzle is a good energizer to get people thinking in non-traditional ways prior to an idea-generation session. See more ideas in Chapter 8.

Focus

Stay Focused as a Participant by Being Prepared and Through Active Listening and Involvement

We have emphasized the roles of initiator, timekeeper, recorder, and especially the facilitator in keeping a meeting focused on its purpose and agenda. What about participants? If participants stay involved in the meeting, the work of every other role is much easier. In many respects, the responsibilities of participants are the most important. Here are some ways for you to prepare as a participant of any meeting:

⇨   Read and absorb materials sent in advance to review.

⇨   Prepare a point of view on key issues—develop questions, ideas, and opinions for the group to consider.

⇨   Determine your goals for the meeting. What do you want to accomplish in the meeting? How will the information or decisions impact your area of responsibility?

⇨   Take the meeting seriously. Show up on time, and stay involved throughout the meeting. If you have other pressing priorities (and who doesn't?), set them aside for the time of the meeting. Be respectful of others by turning off your cell phone, PDA, computer, or other devices.

⇨   Practice active listening during the meeting by concentrating on speakers with your eyes, giving visual and verbal resonse, and fully responding to what is going on.

⇨   When you voice an opinion or concern, know where you are going before you start. Make sure your comments are relevant to the subject being discussed. Don't chime in just to hear yourself talk!

⇨   Learn and practice skills that help maintain group harmony or keep the group on track. (See Chapter 6 for more details.)

ADDITIONAL IDEAS FOR KEEPING MEETINGS FOCUSED

Get in the habit of starting meetings on time. It sends a signal that you respect everyone's time, and sets the right tone for focused, effective meetings. You may have to start with several people not present when you decide to initiate this ground rule. After a few times, most people will make the effort to show up on time. Consider starting at an unusual time, such as 9:13 a.m. or 1:41 p.m. When you start precisely at the announced time, people will get the idea.

One board on which I served held its meetings in members' homes. Because of this, the members spent the first 15 minutes or so of each meeting socializing. Rather than discontinue the social time, we simply established that the social period began at 7 p.m. and started the meeting at 7:15. It worked.

Establish the ground rule of "only one meeting—no side conversations." This helps to keep everyone focused on the topic at hand.

Take a progress check midway through the meeting. Recap agenda items covered, and those remaining. Make any mid-course corrections to keep the meeting focused and accomplish the purpose. The facilitator should do this anytime he or she senses the group needs to get refocused on the purpose of the meeting.

If people arrive after the meeting has begun, refer them to the group notes to get up to date on what has transpired. If you stop the meeting to inform latecomers, it might reinforce their behavior. The simple act of starting every meeting on time will go a long way to discourage latecomers.

In training meetings, stop after a block of information has been covered, usually about 20 minutes or so. Go around the room and ask participants to recap one or two things they learned that will be most helpful to them. This "group summary" will reinforce the learning, and let the trainer know what is being retained. It will also provide a launching point to focus the next training segment.

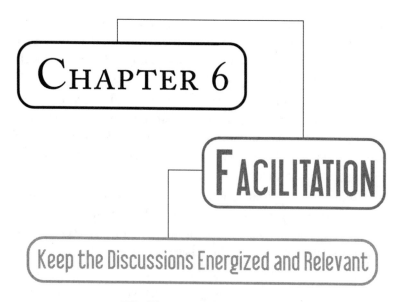

CHAPTER 6

FACILITATION

Keep the Discussions Energized and Relevant

The Truth You Never Hear

"Let's just ramble out of control for the next two hours. Say whatever pops into your mind, whether it's relevant to the topic or not. It won't make any difference anyway, because everyone knows these meetings are a joke. Because no one is in charge, feel free to take control whenever you feel like it."

The Challenges

THE MEETING IS OUT OF CONTROL

Things seem to hum along in the meeting, up to a point. There is a stated purpose, and the group starts out by following an agenda. You may have appointed a timekeeper and recorder. However, there is no one to guide the discussion, keep the group focused, and take charge when the discussion drifts. As a result, the more expressive people get the most "air time," and are able to slant the discussion toward their point of view.

People start telling war stories. Side issues surface. The timekeeper tries his or her best to remind the group that they are running over. More often than we like to admit, the meeting turns into an energy-draining free-for-all, with little accomplished.

By the second hour of a daylong school board retreat, the group sensed that they were in for a wearying session. The president decided to shake things up and not run the meeting as he usually did. Instead, he said he wanted to be a silent observer and simply listen. Because he did not appoint a facilitator, no one was in charge.

The event was a planning retreat for the school board, and the group's task was to come up with ideas that would make the board more responsive to the community and the needs of students. However, because there was no facilitator for the retreat, no ground were rules established, and the meeting stumbled along.

The problem was not preparation. In fact, every board member came prepared to discuss several ideas. At numerous points, it seemed that each person was more interested in making sure his or her ideas were heard and carried out, rather than working toward a common goal. This meant that the discussion often veered off in different directions. Ultimately the result was that the board members were mentally and physically drained midway through the morning of the first day.

This meeting got bogged down and it drifted, like a ship without a captain, or even a rudder. Shortly after lunch, the president called an early end to the retreat, because it was clear that very little was going to be accomplished.

Some Group Members Are Excluded

Some people have attended meetings that become debilitating experiences for them, because they seem to be excluded from the proceedings. The initiator or facilitator seldom calls on them, and it is difficult for them to break into the flow of the conversation. Without a strong sense of feeling included, they may eventually withdraw and generally cannot wait until the meeting is over. Worse, when they finally offer ideas of suggestions, they are often crushed with negative responses, which can make them withdraw even further.

OVER-CONTROLLED MEETINGS

While having a facilitator is generally a good thing, it is possible to take a heavy-handed approach that is more stifling than stimulating. Symptoms of over-controlled meetings include strict adherence to rules, such as parliamentary procedure, initiators, or facilitators who do more talking than listening, and other autocratic behavior. Another problem occurs when facilitators try to micromanage every last detail. Most people do not respond well to over-controlled meetings. They feel manipulated or powerless, and tune out rapidly.

Although a heavy-handed approach to facilitation might seem to be an efficient way to run a meeting, it is clearly not a very effective way to get the group members involved and enthusiastically contributing.

Ideas and Solutions for Facilitation That Works

⇨ Educate all group members in group processes and facilitation skills.

⇨ Encourage all group members to learn and use positive meeting language.

⇨ Designate a facilitator for every meeting.

⇨ Separate the role of meeting initiator from the role of facilitator.

Educate Group Members in Group Processes and Facilitation Skills

Although I have observed several facilitators who are able to lead groups intuitively, most of them do not possess some mystical powers— they have simply taken the time to learn and practice basic skills. Any organization that has meetings will benefit by having a cadre of trained people who are available to facilitate meetings. For ongoing teams and any group that meets regularly, I recommend that every participant learn basic facilitator skills.

A significant benefit of having lots of people trained in group process and facilitation skills is that your meetings will take a quantum leap in effectiveness. The reason? Facilitators also make excellent group partici- pants, because of their keen awareness of the strategies and techniques that make meetings productive. Some of the most enjoyable and productive meetings I have attended or facilitated have occurred when other trained facilitators have attended as participants.

What are the skills that an effective meeting facilitator should learn and refine? My top 10 list includes:

1. The ability to remain neutral and objective throughout the meeting. This means not showing favoritism toward any individuals or ideas.

2. Having high energy and being able to keep the group involved and energized throughout the meeting.

3. Being assertive without being abrasive. This requires sensing when to intervene and when to back off and let things take their course.

4. The ability to listen well, and to know when the meeting is veering off the subject or otherwise not moving to- ward accomplishing its purpose.

5. An unwavering dedication to serving the needs of the group. This includes checking with the initiator and other group members often to confirm that they are satisfied with what is happening, and how their time is being spent. This always means putting the group's interests ahead of any personal interests.

6. The ability to encourage participation among all group members while making each person comfortable. This requires recognizing and honoring the fact that people have different styles of thinking and communicating.

7. The capability to create a safe, open, trusting, and supportive environment for all group members.

8. Being able to recognize and deal with hidden agendas, disruptive behaviors, and potentially explosive situations.

9. Being alert to group "membership" issues, especially for people who are new to the group.

10. Having a gentle sense of humor and knowing when and how to use it effectively in the meeting.

Beyond these general skills are specific group process functions that are designed to maintain good relationships among members, and keep the meeting focused. Although mastering these functions is a must for facilitators, I recommend these skills be learned and practiced by all group members.

Group maintenance functions

These are process skills that build or keep good relationships among members of the group.

⇨ Building and crediting. This involves giving positive reinforcement to group members by adding onto or modifying others' ideas or suggestions. The goal is to recognize the contributions of others while adding a contribution of your own. This is one of the most powerful techniques you can use in meetings.

⇨ Encouraging. This skill means remaining friendly, positive, and responsive to group members and their contributions, without showing favoritism.

⇨ Expressing group feelings. Using this ability means sensing moods, feelings, and relationships in the group, and relieving tension with appropriate use of humor.

⇨ Harmonizing. This means encouraging people to explore their differences and appreciate each other's point of view; for example, suggesting that two people who disagree get together at the break to find a mutually acceptable solution.

⇨ Gatekeeping. This is the ability to encourage participation of all participants by keeping the channels of communication open.

⇨ Observing. An astute observer is aware of the overall process—what is going on in the meeting that helps or hinders the group achieving its purpose. This also includes being aware of physical dynamics such as heat, ventilation, and uncomfortable chairs. At appropriate times, he or she brings the observations to the attention of the group, perhaps suggesting changes.

Task skills

These are process techniques that help keep the group focused on the meeting's purpose.

⇨ Clarifying. This involves carefully listening to and interpreting what is being discussed, and clearing up confusion to make sure that everyone has the same understanding of the issues or ideas. For example, a clarifier may intervene when someone is using jargon that is unfamiliar to some, asking that the terms be explained.

⇨ Summarizing. This skill entails pulling together related ideas, restating issues after the group has discussed them, identifying areas of agreement, and offering a recommendation or conclusion for the group to accept or reject. This is a useful technique to assess the group's progress on the agenda after a break or major segment of the meeting.

⇨ Initiating. An initiator suggests ways for the group to solve a problem, generate ideas, solicit opinions on an issue, or move toward closure.

⇨ Information giving and seeking. Similar to clarifying, the facilitator presents facts or relevant information about issues being discussed; or seeks information and data from others.

⇨ Consensus building and testing. This is the ability to move the group toward common agreement by taking straw votes to identify and isolate the things everyone agrees on, finding ways to resolve differences and come to agreement.

In conducting train-the-facilitator meeting skills seminars, I have observed that it is relatively easy for facilitators to grasp the essentials of group process skills. That said, it requires practice with a healthy dose of trial-and-error to learn the skills, and to know when and how to use them effectively and naturally in "real time" during a meeting.

GETTING STARTED WITH FACILITATOR TRAINING

If anyone in your group has experience as a facilitator or is familiar with the basic skills, ask if he or she would be willing to conduct the initial training for other group members. Other options include sending one or more people to training courses, or bringing in a skilled trainer to conduct in-house train-the-facilitator sessions.

Regardless of the initial training, the best way to learn and reinforce facilitator and group process skills is through practice. Fortunately, your group is likely to have frequent meetings to provide the practice opportunities. New facilitators will need and appreciate the understanding, patience, and tolerance of other group members while they polish their skills.

In the training and practice sessions, appoint one person to be a process observer. This person's job is to observe how interactions are handled in the meeting versus what is actually being discussed. This would include noting when the facilitator and other group members intervene to keep the meeting on track, as well as when they intentionally say or do something to maintain group harmony. Immediately following the practice session, the process observer leads a discussion to share his or her observations with other group members.

Develop and Encourage Positive "Meeting Language"

Positive meeting language is purposeful and empowering to all group members. Eventually each member and facilitator should develop his or her own vocabulary, so it does not sound scripted or contrived. Here are some examples of positive meeting language to get you thinking in the right direction:

Facilitation

Process Skill	Language
Building and crediting	"Hitchhiking on Jane's suggestion of automating the packing, why don't we look at automating the whole process?"
Encouraging	"Terrific concept, Patti. Who can see a way to incorporate this in your department?"
Expressing group feelings	"Our energy is beginning to drag a little—what do you say we take a quick break?"
Harmonizing	"Let's remember that every opinion is valid. Although we all may not agree on everything at first, it is important to get everyone's input. Then we can decide how to proceed."
Gatekeeping	"Tim, because you're new to this division, your observations will be valuable to us…care to comment?"
Observing	"Hey, we did a great job in coming up with some fresh approaches. Good show!"
Clarifying	"Agnes, are you saying that the equipment is unaffordable, or it's just not in this year's budget?"
Summarizing	"Let's take a moment to see where we stand. We have all agreed on (whatever) and have yet to tackle the budget."
Initiating	"Let's go around the room and get everyone's reaction."
Information giving	"My department did a study on that about six months ago. One of the things we found…"

Process Skill	Language
Information seeking	"Does anyone know if our customers think this is important?"
Opinion giving	"This solution would make life easier in my department. Let's work on finding a way to pay for it."
Opinion seeking	"Bob, do you think this would fly with the engineering guys?"
Consensus building and testing	"Let's see where we stand on this. Is there anyone who can't live with the ABC strategy?" or "Is everybody comfortable with this strategy?"
Time management	"Our time is almost up. How do you want to spend the remaining 15 minutes?"
Get meeting on track	"Let's put these side issues in the 'parking lot' for now, and focus on completing the personnel recommendation."
Control disruptive behavior (side conversations)	"Remember our ground rule for one conversation at a time. The recorder won't be able to capture all the ideas if everyone talks at once."

DESIGNATE A FACILITATOR FOR EVERY MEETING

One of the best ways to accelerate a group's progress toward effective meetings is to appoint a facilitator for every meeting. This will provide "on the job" learning opportunities for facilitators-in-training, and will heighten every member's awareness of good meeting skills.

The facilitator role should be rotated among every member who has been trained or is in training. One way to break in people who are new to facilitation is to have them start with handling only a portion of the meeting. For longer meetings, a team facilitating approach works well—break the meeting into segments and have two or more facilitators take turns. This allows one person to rejuvenate while observing or participating in the meeting, while the other person facilitates the meeting. Once group members have experienced the benefits of well-facilitated meetings, they will never want to have a meeting any other way.

SEPARATE FACILITATOR AND INITIATOR ROLES

Many meetings run amok when the initiator, who is the boss or authority figure of the group, also acts as the facilitator for the meeting. This bears repeating here, because of its importance. Initiators naturally have a vested interest in the outcome, which makes it difficult (if not impossible) to fulfill the most important facilitator trait: remaining neutral and objective throughout the meeting.

Here are some additional reasons to separate the roles:

⇨ With a separate facilitator, the initiator is free to contribute information and ideas as a full participant. He or she can also focus on listening to the ideas and contributions of others, without having to be concerned about how the meeting is running.

⇨ While the facilitator is in charge of the meeting process, the initiator is still responsible for the outcome of the meeting. A facilitator is not a decision-maker; he or she is only responsible for running the process of the meeting.

⇨ Participants will open up and contribute more if the initiator/boss is not running the meeting. When people fully participate in the process, they will have a stronger investment in the outcome. A consensus is more likely to emerge from a group whose members are fully engaged.

If the facilitator is in charge of the meeting, what, then, is the role of the initiator? Without having to worry about running the meeting, the initiator is able to listen more and play a part in the meeting as a participant. Although there is no need to be neutral, it is usually best if the initiator listens to input from other group members before expressing his or her own viewpoint. Most initiators who turn over facilitation to others are able to relax more and enjoy the benefits of higher quality and more honest input from group members.

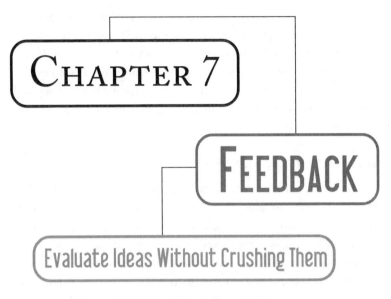

CHAPTER 7

FEEDBACK

Evaluate Ideas Without Crushing Them

The Truth You Never Hear

"Well, we managed to blow off another three hours today with little to show for it, except to learn the latest chapter in Andrea's on-going melodrama with the purchasing department. Most of the other reports were full of the usual buzzwords and jargon, with little real substance. We also managed to kill off every idea that was suggested, in record time. Despite our efforts to go off on as many tangents as possible, we only went an hour and 10 minutes over schedule. We now have eight separate plans of action, narrowed down from the two we started with!"

The Challenges

FACILITATOR/PRESENTERS DO NOT RESPOND TO ONGOING FEEDBACK

Meeting participants send frequent signals that give clues to their level of engagement. If facilitators and presenters do not observe and respond to this ongoing feedback from group members, they are missing a great opportunity to make the meeting more productive and relevant. This kind of feedback, not necessarily spoken out loud yet, "speaks" loudly through body language and eye contact, or the lack of it. Participants who are counting ceiling tiles, examining the inside of their eyelids, or doodling on their pads are sending clear signals. If the group isn't engaged, the presenter or facilitator may find him- or herself talking to the walls before too long.

IDEAS ARE CRUSHED AS THEY ARE OFFERED

Another challenge is dealing with instant negative criticism to ideas. Many potentially useful ideas are left at the starting gate because someone puts them down almost as quickly as they are offered. Many of us are conditioned to respond negatively to the ideas and suggestions of others. Maybe it's because we want to show how smart we are, or we simply wish to assert ourselves. I am convinced that most people do not intend harm when we judge others' ideas—we are simply unaware of what we're doing and the impact it has on others. For many, it is a knee-jerk reaction that is hard to break.

The energy of the room was electric. Hal had asked some of the best and brightest people in the company to attend what he called a "green-light session," to brainstorm ideas for improving customer service. The session was held in a nice resort, and the dress was casual. In fact, it had all the elements for a successful meeting. Everyone came prepared with a collection of ideas related to customer service in their respective areas.

Hal asked each person to share a few ideas to start things off. Jackson was first and suggested that the firm pinpoint its best customers and build better relationships with them by finding out how the company can serve them better. Hal smiled, then answered, "We might be better off focusing on getting new customers, because we should already know what our current customers like." Jackson nodded his head in reluctant agreement, although he confided to Sally later that the company didn't have a clue about the needs of their most important customers.

Maureen suggested a process for trimming order-filling turnaround time from 14 to five days. To implement the new system, computer hardware upgrades and new software would be required. Hal almost leapt out of his chair. "Maureen, we just spent a ton of money last year for new computers, with little to show for it. How can we justify spending even more?" After some discussion, illustrated by excellent backup numbers, she convinced Hal that the company should at least test her idea in one region.

It was Rolf's turn next. He was proud of the homework he had done, leading him to suggest several ideas for improving communications with customers through a newsletter and on-line forum. Hal's response was cordial, but he pointed out that the company tried a newsletter about five years ago, before Rolf's time, and it didn't do any good. Before Rolf could respond, Hal admonished the group: "This is supposed to be a collection of the best thinkers we have in the company. So far, we're not getting very many good ideas. I hope the rest of you come up with something better."

The meeting dragged on for several painful hours. Hal immediately critiqued every idea that was suggested, and most of his feedback was disapproving. After a while most group members felt very uncomfortable, and simply stopped offering any more ideas. One by one everyone closed down, and they were all relieved when this "brainstorming" retreat was over. If this was a green-light session, maybe Hal was colorblind!

The problem with giving "instant" negative responses to ideas is three-fold:

> ⇨   Ideas die in their infancy, and many good ones will be lost forever.

⇨ People tend to shut down when their ideas get crushed, and may even become hostile, or attempt to thwart the purpose of the meeting.

⇨ The number of ideas is greatly reduced when each is evaluated as it is offered. It is a little like driving while riding the brakes.

No Procedure to Evaluate, Sort, and Prioritize the Best Ideas

How many times have you been in a meeting at which dozens or even hundreds of ideas are generated, only to learn later that no attempts were made to sort out which ideas were best, and ultimately no action was taken? Although generating ideas needs to be separated from evaluating them, eventually ideas must be sorted out, evaluated, and prioritized. Without evaluation, ideas and thought-starters fizzle, and don't become solutions to the problems or issues.

Ideas and Solutions for Feedback and Evaluation

⇨ Observe verbal and non-verbal feedback during the meeting, and respond accordingly.

⇨ Separate creating ideas from evaluating ideas.

⇨ Learn the language of positive feedback and how to give a balanced response when evaluating ideas and suggestions.

⇨ Develop constructive ways to sort out and prioritize the best ideas.

Feedback

Observe Feedback During the Meeting and Respond Accordingly

One thing that keeps meetings interesting, relevant, and productive is for the facilitator and presenters to constantly monitor feedback from the group members and respond accordingly. Verbal feedback is fairly easy to interpret—the nature of questions and comments will usually indicate how well group members are absorbing the content. Non-verbal clues are more subtle. These include observing body language, sleepy eyes, people looking out the window or reading unrelated material, or checking e-mails or cell phone messages. I am amazed at how many speakers deliver a presentation without sensing and adjusting their delivery to respond to the feedback that people give so freely.

Responding to feedback can take many forms, ranging from small adjustments to major interventions. For example, if it appears that the group is not comprehending complex information, the facilitator or presenter can check with participants to see if further explanation is needed. One way to do this is to simply ask members for their interpretation, or open up a discussion to the whole group. In this way, group members will add more specific verbal feedback to their non-verbal signals. I recommend frequent check-ins to make sure group members are onboard, before moving on to a new subject.

Other techniques facilitators and presenters can use to respond to feedback during the meeting include calling a break, summarizing decisions or actions, introducing a game or energizer, or changing the mode of presentation.

Separate Idea Generation From Evaluation

One of the fundamental principles of brainstorming established by Alex Osborn more than a half century ago is to separate the process of generating ideas from evaluating them. To be clear, not all ideas are original, useful, or creative—especially when first offered. However, ideas that are crushed in infancy never have a chance. By encouraging ideas to flow without first evaluating them, they are given a chance to incubate and flourish. The longer ideas are kept alive, the more they begin to grow on people and capture their imagination. Soon, others begin to appreciate them and suggest ways to improve the ideas by building and shaping them with ideas and enhancements of their own.

Kelly had been quiet for much of the council meeting, which was centered on ways to reenergize the church's lagging capital funds campaign. She was the newest member of the council, and was a naturally shy person. At one point, she said, "What if we borrow the money from ourselves?"

The recorder wrote, "Borrow from ourselves" on the flip chart along with all the other ideas. The council was in the midst of a free-flow of ideas, and this was one of many. A little later, Fred said: "I'd like to return to the idea of borrowing from ourselves. What did you have in mind, Kelly?" Kelly explained her idea in more detail. She wondered if it would be possible to bypass the banks by asking members to loan money directly to the church. Chuck said he remembered reading about a company that specialized in underwriting bond issues for churches, but couldn't remember the details.

After a quick search on the Internet, information from several bond underwriters was found, and two firms were contacted. Within three months, the church completed a highly successful bond drive to raise the funds necessary for the parish hall renovation. The bond issue sold out in less than a week, with church members buying the entire issue. Indeed, they borrowed the money from themselves, all because Kelly's idea was given a chance to grow and flourish. What do you suppose might have happened if someone responded to Kelly by saying, "What are you, crazy? We're not millionaires!"

Separating idea generating from evaluating will greatly increase the number of ideas generated. If your goal was to come up with six options for a problem, wouldn't you rather choose from dozens of alternatives or only a few? Original ideas or thought-starters may be partly developed concepts, or even totally unworkable off-the-wall notions. By simply recording ideas without evaluating them as they occur, one thought sparks another and eventually workable solutions begin to emerge. This is when meetings become stimulating and fun!

However, separating the two processes doesn't, mean ignoring the flaws in ideas. It simply means withholding judgment until lots of ideas from the group are on the table, before switching into the evaluation mode.

LEARN THE LANGUAGE OF POSITIVE FEEDBACK AND BALANCED RESPONSES

How do you feel when someone puts down one of your ideas? The effect of negative responses is dramatic. Idea busters or killer phrases do more than squash a particular idea—they often send a message to group members that their ideas are not welcome, especially if the judgment comes from the boss or another senior person.

We are often not conscious of how devastating our cynical judgments can be. The first step is for group members to increase their attentiveness to negative responses that crush ideas. Once a person becomes aware, it is not too difficult to develop new reactions that transform harsh impulses into words of encouragement. The following list compares judgments that crush ideas (Idea Busters) with language that encourages ideas (Idea Builders).

Idea Busters	Idea Builders
It just doesn't grab me.	Tell me more.
We tried that before and it didn't work.	What's different now and what can we change to make it work?
It's been done to death.	Let's do it better (or differently).

Idea Busters	Idea Builders
We can't afford that.	What are some ways we can find the money to try this?
Don't fight the system.	Let's change the system.
We've never done anything like that.	This is exciting stuff!
The boss will never buy it.	How can we sell it to the boss?
That's really off the wall.	How could we test your idea?
Oh??	Yes! Let's try it.
The timing isn't right.	Let's work out the best timing.
The last guy who suggested that isn't here anymore.	What if it were possible?
I like my idea better.	Let's combine our ideas to get the best solution.
That only solves half the problem.	Let's isolate what works and then focus on the concerns.
We need something more exciting.	How can we add excitement?
Great idea, but not for us.	Great idea—let's see if we can make it fit (work) for us.
Where'd you get that idea?	Bravo! Great thinking!
It'll never work (fly, sell).	How can we make it work?
I have a better idea...	Building on your idea...
That is so lame.	Good start—who can build on it?
What will the board (committee) say?	Let's make sure we address the board's (committee's) concerns
Yes, but...	Yes, and...
I don't agree.	I agree with (x and y) and need help in understanding (z).

Feedback

Use the balanced response technique

Many people erroneously think that evaluating ideas means exposing what is wrong with them. The problem with that common approach is that it often throws out the good with the bad. Few ideas are totally worthless, and rarely are they perfect either, especially when first formulated. A more productive way to evaluate ideas (suggestions, concepts, and so on) is to identify and preserve the strengths while looking for ways to overcome the flaws and concerns. One proven technique to extract the "good stuff" from ideas and find ways to make them work is the balanced response. This is based on answering with itemized responses, a technique used in the Synectics creative problem-solving methodology.

Similar to the $+/\triangle$ (plus/delta) process for debriefing meetings, here is how it works: Identify at least three positives about the idea or concept, such as its function, strategic fit, affordability, appeal, or whatever else you like about it. Capture these on a flip chart, computer, or piece of paper. Then identify and write any flaws or concerns using speculative language, such as "how can we…" or, "how to…" or, "I wish…"

To illustrate using the balanced response technique, let's say a private school wants to explore using its classrooms during the summer. The challenge is stated as "How to increase classroom use in the summer months." In a brainstorm meeting, one idea offered is to air-condition the school. (We are assuming our group did not crush the idea with something like, "That's absurd, it will cost a fortune!") Using the balanced response technique to evaluate this idea, the positives are identified:

⇨ We could schedule adult education courses all summer long.

⇨ We could use classrooms for inter-generation summer camp activities.

⇨ Teachers and students would be more comfortable (and productive) in the warmer months, for example, September and May–June.

⇨ We might be able to use the heating ducts, saving money.

Then the concerns are identified:

⇨ Affordability (stated as: "How can we pay for it?").

　➡ Are adult education or other programs viable? ("I wish we knew…")

　➡ How can we find out whether or not the heating ducts can be used?

　➡ The balanced response forces the group to identify and isolate the suitable parts and then focus on the concerns—the parts that need work—describing each concern as a problem to be solved.

　➡ In the example, "How can we pay for it?" becomes a new challenge or problem to be solved, causing the group to generate specific ideas. These might include:

⇨ Holding fundraising events or a bond drive.

⇨ Buying a reconditioned system.

⇨ Finding sponsors.

Addressing the second concern ("I wish we knew if adult education programs were viable") ideas might include:

⇨ Running a test program during the fall.

⇨ Sending a questionnaire to probe interest from a sample of the community.

As the group works through and builds ideas that address the concerns, the original idea is transformed into a possible solution, ranked with other alternatives. Often, concerns crop up in the areas of cost or implementation. For example, "That's a great idea, but where are we going to get the money?" By identifying and isolating the strengths of an idea, then focusing on the concerns, treating them as "how can we" rather than "we can't," any idea becomes possible until all avenues for improving it have been exhausted.

The balanced response technique is a powerful method to refine good ideas that might otherwise be lost. People are empowered when their ideas are respected and developed. When groups are asked to evaluate ideas generated by others, some kind of system is useful to prevent good ideas from going down in flames. The balanced response is one of several ways to keep the conversation constructive and build ideas to a point at which they can be against others to select the best.

LEARN HOW TO REFINE, SORT OUT, AND PRIORITIZE IDEAS

Building ideas using the balanced response or other techniques helps ensure they are given a chance. The process does not stop there, however. Ideas must be refined, sorted, and prioritized, so the group is able to choose the best solution.

The WEIRD technique for refining ideas

One technique that I use with groups to build and refine ideas uses the acronym WEIRD. Each person starts with a blank piece of paper and writes per the instructions that follow. After each round, papers are passed to the right, and everyone continues writing, building on the ideas written on the paper they receive. If your meeting is being conducted electronically, use a collaborative software program (also known as groupware) that allows simultaneous input from all participants. Limit each round to no more than two minutes.

⇒   **Wild**—Using the "problem as stated" or initial idea, think of as many off-the-wall ideas and solutions as possible. The goal is quantity. Encourage people not to self-evaluate as they let their creative juices flow. (Remember to write legibly!)

⇨ **Enhance**—In this round, participants use the "wild" ideas in front them as springboards, and add enhancements to improve on them. The focus remains on creativity, without worrying about practicality at this point.

⇨ **Insight**—This round calls for some discernment. Each person now has a sheet with ideas and enhancements from two rounds—the task is to find a promising idea or insight from the collection, or that is stimulated from the list, perhaps by combining one or more thoughts into a single concept. Write this idea on the paper and circle it.

⇨ **Refine**—In this round, participants polish the idea handed to them into a workable concept or solution for the issue at hand. This might include using the balanced response technique to sort out pluses and identify concerns, and offering additional thoughts to address them.

⇨ **Defend**—In the final round, the idea is fully expressed, including developing a well-thought-out "defense" on why the idea has merit.

Here are some methods that can be used to select and prioritize ideas:

⇨ **Quick Sort**. This approach requires group members to place ideas into one of several categories in order to sort them. For example, categories might include: (1) Winners—implement immediately; (2) Needs Work—find a way; (3) Incubate; and (4) Not now. Make up your own categories if you wish, and keep them positive. Imagine how you would feel if your idea was thrown into a category labeled "Dogs." Remember that a certain idea might not be the answer for today's challenge, but it might provide the pathway to another idea or solution tomorrow. The Quick Sort technique can be easily done via computer by using the outline view in a word processing program.

⇨ **Dot Voting.** Use this method when a large number of ideas are written on flip charts, and hung around the room. All group members are given three to 10 self-adhesive colored dots to place next to ideas that they feel are best—either based on judgment (do they like them?) or against specified criteria. At the end of the process, the winning ideas will be visually apparent to all; simply add up the ideas with the most dot votes, and rank them. Recognize that the dot voting method only reflects the input of the people voting. It does, however, provide a quick and fun way to get instant feedback from the group, and it virtually guarantees consensus, because everyone is voting the same way. Groups asked to evaluate ideas generated by others also may do dot voting. Indeed, dot voting is a useful way to trim any list to a manageable number.

⇨ **Rate versus Criteria.** After ideas have been whittled down to a manageable number, it is often useful to choose the "best of the best." Rating ideas against specific criteria is one way to do this. Criteria used should stem from the objectives and strategies you have established. For example, if the goal is to generate new product ideas for snack products targeted at teens, criteria might include:

1. Appeal to teens.
2. Technology available.
3. Innovative packaging.
4. Bring to market in one year.
5. Offers competitive insulation.

Alternative ideas or concepts may simply be checked off against these standards or rated on a numerical scale (for example 1–5 or 1–10) on how well they meet the criteria. A refinement of this method is to assign a point value to each of the criteria, based on importance. Then, rate the ideas on how well they meet the criteria. Multiply the ratings times the point value and add up the results. See the following example:

CRITERIA	VALUE (1–10)	IDEA # 1 (TOT)	IDEA # 2 (TOT)	IDEA # 3 (TOT)
Appeal to teens	9	6 (54)	8 (72)	4 (36)
Technology avail.	7	4 (28)	6 (42)	9 (63)
Packaging	5	9 (45)	2 (10)	7 (35)
Market one year	6	2 (12)	4 (24)	6 (36)
Total rating		139	148	170

The value of methods such as Quick Sort, Dot Voting, and Rating versus Criteria is that they easily measure the consensus of the group. From this point, additional evaluation or research might be needed to confirm the group's opinion.

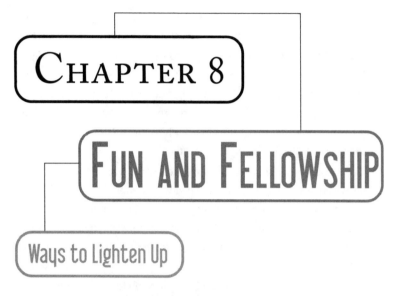

CHAPTER 8

FUN AND FELLOWSHIP

Ways to Lighten Up

The Truth You Never Hear

"For the next two hours, we are going to ask that you resist your natural impulses to laugh out loud when something strikes you as funny. In fact, even giggles and smirks will be looked on with disdain. We're about serious business here, and having fun is clearly inconsistent with our meeting purpose. Our goal is to generate some new approaches for reducing employee turnover. Now let's get going with some really creative ideas."

The Challenges

TAKING OURSELVES TOO SERIOUSLY

If we could review videos of some of the meetings we have attended, I suspect many of us would grimace at how terribly pragmatic and serious they are. We might also notice that whenever laughter broke out amidst the boredom, it often became a catalyst for relieving pressure and making progress in the group. Humor often helps us cut through the titles, the posturing, and the positions that limit our thinking and stifle participation.

Naturally, we should take our work seriously—it's what we get paid to do, or what we have agreed to do as a volunteer committee member. What happens all too often, however, is that we take ourselves too seriously. We get wrapped up in our self-importance, and somehow think we have to always act seriously now that we have the title of vice-president, manager, committee head, or project leader.

The result of all this seriousness often spills over into meetings. It seems wrong somehow to have fun when we are supposed to be working. So we stifle playfulness and laughter, and instead hold boring, humorless meetings. When humor is used positively, most of us appreciate the lightness it brings to a meeting. Used properly, humor can greatly enhance the work output of meetings.

When presenting to the board of directors of (former conglomerate) American Brands, my purpose was to convey that our foods division was innovative and forward thinking. We were presenting a bold recommendation for reducing our product line from more than 400 items to about 70, in order to concentrate on the best-selling, most profitable items. Although the business case was strong, our plan would require a significant write-off for inventory of discontinued items, which would be expensive in the first year. The night before the presentation, I was helping to repair a few of my daughter's broken dolls at home, and got an inspiration for a visual aid.

The presentation seemed to go well, and I purposely left out any reference to the cost of the inventory write-off. The CEO ("Chairman Bob") made a few supportive comments. Then he leaned back in his chair, took a puff on his cigar, and asked what our recommendation would cost. Somewhat cautiously, I pulled out my prop, which was a poster with a doll's arm and a leg attached, from the spare parts box, of course. Holding up the visual, I looked the Chairman Bob straight in the eye and said, "It's not going to be cheap, Bob…it's going to cost you an arm and a leg!" The stunned board members were silent until the chairman cracked a little smile, which widened into a grin and then into laughter. Soon, everyone appreciated not only my humor, but also the boldness of our approach. The meeting turned into a lively discussion of the pros and cons of the proposal, with little regard for power, position, or any of the other barriers.

Is there a risk in using humor? I suppose I could have been fired for such an approach. Fortunately, I had done some research on Chairman Bob and discovered that he appreciated both directness and a good laugh. Even with that information, I did not decide to use my audacious visual aid until I read the feedback both from the chairman and others in the meeting. The risk was definitely worth it. And yes, the proposal was approved.

Not Enough Variety = Boring Meetings

We have mentioned ways in which potentially exciting meetings can become boring: unclear purpose, wrong people in the meeting, lack of preparation, wandering from the agenda, and others. Another way to almost guarantee tedium is to limit the ways in which information is delivered or discussed. This includes allowing one person to talk too long, handling all agenda items in the same way, and using look-alike visual aids for all presentations. Too much of anything is never a good thing. For example, five to 15 minutes of a well-produced video or film clip can bring life and zest to a meeting, while a two-hour video on any subject is likely to become boring at some point, no matter how well produced. I probably have a shorter attention span than many, so I am aware of my bias in this area. Nonetheless, I have observed many group members throughout the years drift into "Never-Never Land" midway through meetings, because there was not enough variety to keep them interested and involved.

Group Members Do Not Know Each Other

This challenge occurs in newly formed groups, and with people who do not normally meet together. I have also seen it happen in groups that have been meeting for months or years. There is a limit to the productivity of meetings if group members do not know each other on a personal level. When there is no disclosure or intimacy, people tend to talk at one another rather than with each other. Although the type of group and purpose of the meeting determine degree of familiarity, it usually enriches the meeting in many ways.

From my experience in coaching graduate business students from many countries, I have also learned that other cultures value familiarity far more than North Americans, especially in Asian and Hispanic countries. Many American business people have learned the hard way that they need to invest time in building relationships with foreign business associates before charging into a fact-oriented, fast-paced presentation or negotiation. Without knowing anything about the other people in a meeting, participants have to make assumptions as they attempt to discuss, collaborate, and make decisions.

Strategies and Solutions for Boring Meetings

⇨   Lighten up and encourage humor and fun in your meetings.

⇨   Use a number of different formats and techniques to inject variety and to keep things interesting.

⇨   Use games, exercises, and other techniques to enable group members to know one another better and build fellowship.

Lighten Up and Encourage Humor

Learn to include humor in your meetings. It can be as simple as starting out the meeting by asking participants to share something humorous that happened in their departments, or sharing an appropriate cartoon. (Do you ever notice how Dilbert shows up in your office with regularity?) In Chapter 6, we noted that a useful skill for facilitators is a good sense of humor. There is, however, a distinction between humor and comedy. Professionals get paid to do comedy, and they work hard at their material and delivery. Instead, what we're talking about is finding the humor in everyday situations, and observing and reflecting on the absurdity of events, people, and circumstances. Real life is usually funnier than prepared comedy material anyway.

Professional speakers and trainers have long known that wrapping serious messages in relevant anecdotal humor not only makes a more interesting and palatable presentation, but it improves retention as well. In meetings, sharing funny stories about work-related subjects helps everyone relax and builds positive energy.

Be aware that it is possible for humor to backfire. Inappropriate humor, such as sarcasm, can detract from an important discussion, or demean someone who is trying hard to understand something. And, like most things, too much humor is too much. Certainly, ethnic, racist, or sexist comments have no place in meetings. One healthy habit to nurture is the ability to laugh at yourself, because, of course, humans are not perfect. A bit of self-deprecating humor is especially refreshing when it comes from the boss.

Other ways to include fun in your meetings are games, energizers, and exercises, many of which are covered in this chapter and in other parts of this book. Sometimes a simple humorous observation can break the tension and make a profound difference in the direction of a meeting.

My boss Jack and I were reviewing potential design firms to redesign the packaging graphics on several food products. A number of piecemeal changes had been made to the products through the years. Although each change had probably been made for good reason, the line did not stand out among its competitors on grocery store shelves. In fact, the whole array resembled a patchwork quilt rather than a unified product line. Because Jack and I were both fairly new to the company, we carried none of the history and baggage of our predecessors. We were open to dramatic change, unlike our forerunners, who were reputed to be conservative about packaging designs.

During a meeting with one design firm, we noted that there was a considerable amount of posturing and hedging going on among the designers about the current line. This particular firm had done some of the previous work, and they were not sure if either of us had a vested interest in the present designs. At one point, Jack, who was the vice president of marketing at our firm, interrupted and observed, "What you're really saying is that we have a screaming disaster here!"

After gulping and looking at each other, the two designers answered tentatively, "Well, in a word, yes."

Then we smiled, and Jack said, "We agree!" Everyone had a good laugh, and we finally began to talk about the real issues and possible solutions in an open, candid manner.

Learn to laugh, and cultivate an environment that allows and encourages everyone to have a little fun while setting about the serious task of accomplishing your goals.

Use a Variety of Formats and Techniques for Fun, Variety, and Interest

Here are some ways to maintain interest and involvement—and fun—in meetings:

⇨ Change some aspect of the meeting about every 20 to 30 minutes. Incorporate a mix of stimuli, such as solo presentations, group discussions, question-and-answer sessions, small group breakouts (see below), videos, panels, team presentations, individual and group idea generation, voting, exercises, and games.

⇨ Break a large group (more than eight) into smaller groups often for collaboration, discussion, and brainstorming. Have each group report back to the larger group. This does not have to be done in separate rooms. In fact, there is an advantage to holding breakouts in the large meeting room—the buzz and energy are stimulating.

⇨ Hold a stand-up meeting. Few people will fall asleep, and the meeting will probably be much shorter. If the recorder takes notes on a flip chart, no one else has to.

Many organizations schedule stand-up meetings with great success. (See Chapter 3.)

⇨ Make visual aids more graphic. Pictures, drawings, charts, and graphs communicate many concepts quicker and more effectively than words and bullet points on a page.

⇨ Change the meeting environment, just for the fun of it. Meet outside on a nice day, or hold a brunch meeting. Meet by e-mail, live chat, video conference, or audio conference. (See more on electronic meetings in Chapter 14.)

⇨ Change the media for visual support of presentations. Mix computer slides, Internet pages, videos, live props, flip charts, and handouts to add variety and interest.

⇨ Encourage people who make a lot of presentations to take a course to improve their skills. The best ones are laboratory-type seminars that use video feedback to record practice presentations and provide coaching.

⇨ Take two-minute breaks to change the pace and recharge everyone. Ask someone who works with a personal trainer or attends exercise classes to lead the group in a brief stretch or exercise.

⇨ Use a process such as mind mapping—a visual way to capture and express complex ideas—for idea generation, process evaluation, and to enhance both self-expression and communication. Invented by Tony Buzan in the 1960s, mind maps can be drawn on a plain piece of paper or flip chart, or created electronically with the assistance of various free, shareware, or licensed products. A Google search of "mind mapping" will point you in the right direction.

⇨ Use brainteasers, puzzles, or quizzes at the beginning or anytime during a meeting to provide stimulation, a fun discourse, and warm-ups for brainstorming.

⇨ Have someone make a list of all the jargon used in a meeting, and then read it back to the group at the end. Ask yourselves what "real people" (or aliens) would think if they were to be observers during such a meeting.

⇨ Throw a Nerf ball or other soft object at anyone who criticizes or negates an idea during a brainstorming session. The person who has the ball can then throw it at the next naysayer. This is a harmless, fun way to reinforce the ground rules.

Use Games and Exercises to Enhance Fun and Fellowship

In most areas of life, as soon as you learn more about a person, you begin to relate to him or her differently. If you learn that Bill had spent 15 years in engineering, you might understand why and how he is able to come up with quick answers to highly technical challenges. When you learn of Stephanie's struggles raising four children, you begin to appreciate her insights to your product's target market of young mothers. Knowing Bert's background in banking adds credibility to his comments on your board's quarterly financial statements.

Sharing personal information has value in any group. The extent to which group members disclose their histories depends partly on the type of group. Spiritual exploration groups are at one end of the spectrum, whereas business groups obviously are at the other end. Before you dismiss the value of personal disclosure, consider trying it and see what happens in the group. I run monthly business round tables as a chair for Vistage International, and have learned that personal disclosure in a confidential business setting adds real value to the discussions.

For example, in one volunteer group meeting we took a minute or two for each person to "check in" with the rest of the group, sharing a little about what had brought them joy or frustration since we last met. When facilitating idea-generation groups for any type of organization, one of the first things I do is have group members introduce each other with some personal information, such as their favorite hobby or what they were known for in high school. When selecting methods to get to know one another, look for exercises that delve beyond jobs or titles to who the real person is, and how they think and act outside the work or organizational situation.

One of my favorite icebreaker exercises is "Two Truths and a Lie." Each person is asked to tell the group three things about him- or herself that others probably wouldn't know. Everyone is asked to dig into their past or present and come up with something that will challenge the group. Examples: "I was a high school cheerleader," "My wife is a funeral director," "I ran in three marathons races," "My passion is playing chess [or skiing, singing, or making model airplanes.]" "I collect rare coins."

Then the twist: One of the "facts" must be a lie. After the three statements are revealed (one person at a time), the other group members try to guess which one is the lie. The result is that group members learn some interesting information about each other...and they also learn who is good at telling a lie! When everyone gets into the spirit, this is a fun exercise that gets the meeting off to a great start.

In one meeting, we were in the midst of this exercise when a latecomer arrived. I asked him to make out a nametag and quickly explained what we were doing. When his turn came, we tried to guess which one of his statements was the lie. It turned out that none of them were lies...all of the statements were truthful. Reading his nametag, I said: "Mark, what's the lie?" He replied, "My name is Stan, not Mark." The group was off to a great start. Later, we used Stan's (a.k.a. Mark) example to make the point that sometimes you have to break the rules.

Here are some additional games and exercises you can use to break the ice and make it comfortable for people to share personal information.

➪ Have group members pair off and share some personal history for a minute or so each. You might suggest specific questions, such as asking about their major in college, or favorite leisure activities. Then, have each person introduce his or her partner, recalling as much information as they remember. This exercise also builds listening skills.

➪ Ask group members to imagine what they would do if they won the lottery and found themselves $90 million richer. They should describe their dreams. This fantasy excursion reveals dreams, goals, and motivations.

➪ Have group members draw their favorite animal when they were kids, then share it in the large group, or with one other person. Even more fun, have them draw with their non-dominant hand.

➪ Ask group members, "Which actor/actress (living or dead) would you choose to play you in a movie of your life? Explain why." Do this in groups of two or three, then share in the large group.

➪ Start the meeting by having each person share something at work or home that has been very satisfying, plus something that has been frustrating.

➪ Go around the room at the beginning of the meeting and ask each person what his or her expectations are for the meeting. Write these headlines on a flip chart sheet and post it. This exercise is a good way for the initiator, facilitator, and other group members to learn what each person expects to accomplish. This exercise works especially well in training sessions and in strategic planning meetings and retreats.

⇨ Go around the room and have each person complete the sentence: "When I was 17 years old…" This might be a recollection of memories from high school, summer jobs, being in love, or whatever comes to mind.

⇨ Ask each person to identify his or her hero or heroine, and tell the group members why that person is admired. Similarly, invite group members to imagine meeting one person whom they admire, then describe the dream meeting. To build on this, suggest that they would be able to ask this person one question—what would the question be?

⇨ Ask each group member to share how life would be different if humans did not need to sleep (or some other twist). Ask each to further expand on how this would affect his or her life.

⇨ Ask everyone to reflect on their friends, and describe the qualities that make those friends special.

The previous exercises, and many similar ones, can be done one-on-one, in groups of three or four, or in larger groups. Time may be a factor in deciding how to structure the exercise. For example, in a group of 20 people, a big chunk of time can be consumed if each person talks for two or three minutes in the large group. Small group breakouts allow everyone to participate comfortably, without having to be "on stage" in the larger group.

In addition to games and exercises, consider allowing some unstructured social time before or after the meeting, or during a break. The more people know about each other, the better they will relate to each other in meetings. For longer meetings such as conferences and retreats, an informal get-together the night before the meeting starts is a good way for participants to learn a little bit about each other. It will make a significant difference in the meeting the next day.

If you are in an organization with a training department, or hire training consultants from time to time, ask some of the trainers to share a few of the games and energizers they use to perk up training sessions. Many of these can be highly effective to liven up your meetings.

Recap of Part II

Planning a meeting makes provides the foundation for success. Working the plan makes the meeting flow. Implement the 4 F's:

1. *Focus:* Get everybody onboard with the purpose, follow the prioritized agenda, record ideas on the group memory, and manage time.

2. *Facilitation:* Use a facilitator for each meeting, and encourage all participants to learn and use effective meeting skills.

3. *Feedback:* Respond to ongoing feedback and learn constructive ways to evaluate ideas and build them into solutions.

4. *Fun and Fellowship:* Lighten up your meetings with laughter and humor, and get to know each other as people.

PART III

AT THE END AND AFTER THE MEETING

The 4 C's of Completion

CONSENSUS

Make clear decisions that everyone can live with and support.

CLOSURE

Establish clear action steps, timetables, and responsibilities. End on time.

CRITIQUE AND CELEBRATION

Evaluate what was accomplished and the effectiveness of the process. Affirm everyone's contribution.

COMMUNICATION

Make a permanent record of the meeting output and distribute it to participants and others. Follow up to keep projects on track.

133

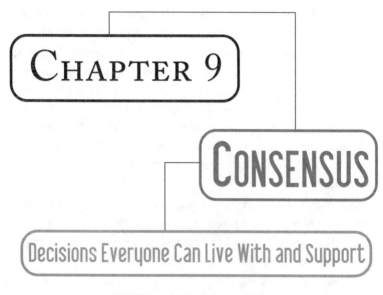

CHAPTER 9

CONSENSUS

Decisions Everyone Can Live With and Support

The Truth You Never Hear

"We've accomplished a great deal in our meeting today…the group has generated tons of great ideas. I suppose it would be a good idea to get the group's opinion on which ones will work best. But instead, we'll just end the meeting now and leave everybody in the dark. I'll probably sit on these ideas for a few weeks, and then make the decision myself."

The Challenges

No Decisions Are Made

The meeting is winding down, and participants are congratulating themselves—deservedly so—after an intense idea-generation session has produced several exciting alternatives. Sadly, many meetings end at this point, with no discernment of which ideas are best, or clarity on what the next steps are. Even if options and possible solutions have been evaluated for strengths, and weaknesses and the most promising ones have been prioritized, nothing will happen until specific action decisions are made regarding which options will be implemented, researched further, or forwarded for approval—in other words, who will do what, by when.

There are many reasons why decisions do not get made. Perhaps there is no sense of urgency, or group members may know that any "decision" they make is really only a recommendation, which has to be approved at a higher level. Most task-oriented meetings cry out for action decisions, yet most of us have attended meetings that have simply ended, with many things left up in the air. Some meetings end with no decisions made, because it is clear that the boss—whether or not he or she is present—will make them later.

Of course, making decisions is not necessary for some types of meetings. The group is not required to make decisions in social meetings, motivational meetings, team building, and other training, and meetings to give or receive information.

However, even social groups must make decisions on such things as when and where the next meeting will be, what the program or agenda will be, and who will be responsible for preparation and logistics. Simple as it may sound, many groups have found difficulty in making decisions of this type.

My wife and I were members of a book group that met once a month. Its purposes included fellowship, enlightenment, and learning. The main activities centered around selecting books and discussing reflections on them. Group members in rotation led the discussions.

As I reflect on this wonderful group, it is amusing to realize just how much time we spent talking about the books we would read, and the formats we would use to review and reflect on them. We spent inordinate amounts of time talking about these issues, sometimes spending more time on them than actually discussing the current book. We began to make some headway when we devoted most of one meeting to selecting books, leaders, and formats six months in advance. With the administrative details planned, the meetings were centered on reflecting on the book for the month.

CONSENSUS APPEARS IMPOSSIBLE

Many initiators and facilitators are intentional about seeking everyone's point of view, and trying to reach consensus. Ultimately, they realize that getting everyone to agree on everything not only takes a long time, it is nearly impossible. When a true consensus decision cannot be reached, participants and leaders are frustrated, and resort to other methods of decision-making.

AUTOCRATIC DECISIONS

Autocratic decisions—those made by one person—are usually faster and easier than collaborative decisions made in a group. Managers and leaders make "solo" decisions every day. Depending on the situation or urgency, an autocratic decision may be the only sensible course of action.

If one's mind is already made up, there is no need to call a meeting to seek the ideas and input of others. Indeed, it is disingenuous to go through the motions of seeking input and encouraging collaboration, only to disregard the suggestions and thoughts of the group.

The greater risk of making autocratic decisions, however, is that there might be little or no support from the group for the ultimate decision if their input was ignored.

A large telephone mail-order center asked me to facilitate a series of employee focus group meetings. The purpose was to get input for the human resources department and top management for structuring employee benefits, and to get a sense of current employee attitudes toward the company. The larger issue was that turnover among phone center employees was substantially higher than the industry average.

During the focus group meetings, I detected a strong sense of resentment from employees toward their supervisors and management. Many were hesitant about participating in a session of this type, fearing that any negative comments might be used against them, although I made it clear that I was an outside contractor. I assured participants of anonymity, and was able to elicit some useful information. Even then, some group members were skeptical that management would take any action on their suggestions.

As it turned out, management did take action, but it was inconsistent with what employees recommended in the focus groups. This served to confirm the employees' suspicions. I often wonder why the management invested the time and money to get employee feedback if they never intended to act on the results. Turnover in the call center remained high.

VOTING

Decisions are made in all kinds of groups by voting. Although a voting process may be better than making no decision, it is often not the best way to keep all group members "whole" and totally committed to the outcome. Why? The simple act of voting to make decisions sets up a win/lose situation: those who vote with the majority "win" and those who do not "lose." It seems fair; after all, it is the democratic process. *Robert's Rules of Order* (DeCapo Press, 2004), parliamentary procedures, and its many variations have conditioned us to think that majority voting is the best way to make a decision in a group. All in favor?

Here's the rub: nobody really likes to lose, no matter how close the vote. As a result, the "losers"—even if only a few people—may try to undermine the group decision, perhaps with others who did not attend the meeting. Those who did not vote with the majority may have unresolved issues, and, if so, will not strongly support the outcome. Depending on the closeness of the vote and the emotional intensity, decisions made by voting could split the group and cause permanent damage to its effectiveness.

Another problem with voting is that it tends to be seen as up/down or black/white. A simple yes or no does not tell you how far apart members are in their views. Are those who vote "no" adamant in their opposition, or perhaps concerned only about a few minor issues? Are the "yes" voters solidly behind the proposition or just barely so? For most issues, there are grey areas, which need to be aired and validated.

GROUPTHINK

The meeting is going well. Almost immediately after the major problem is identified, the boss suggests a solution. Most group members quickly agree that it is a great idea, an obvious solution. Several aspects of the idea strike Georgiana as being impractical, based on her experience. However, she senses that she may be the only person with concerns, and that discussion is not welcome. Georgiana chooses not to rock the boat, and keeps quiet. As a result, the decision is made. Several weeks after it is implemented, fatal flaws were found that proved to be very costly…the very concerns Georgiana had sensed. Welcome to the syndrome of groupthink.

DECISIONS THAT DON'T "STICK"

After a robust discussion, the group comes to agreement on several decisions for a new product rollout that everyone strongly supports. Three days later, however, they find out that the senior vice president, who was not present at the meeting, has "second thoughts," and asks that the rollout plan be reviewed again.

This often happens when the right players are not present in critical meetings, or when the level of authority for the group has not been clearly defined. As a result, many hours can be wasted with little to show for it.

Solutions and Ideas for Building Consensus and Making Decisions That Stick

⇨   Build consensus throughout the meeting, and make decisions that everyone can live with and support.

⇨   Avoid groupthink by inviting healthy discussion and increasing diversity in your meetings.

⇨   Make sure the right people are present in the meeting, and that the level of authority for the group has been clearly defined.

BUILDING CONSENSUS

Total consensus is nearly impossible, because, by definition, it means that everyone agrees absolutely with every aspect of the issue or decision. Getting any two people to absolutely agree on anything is difficult, and, in a group, it's nearly impossible. However, the ability to work to "modified consensus" is the sign of a highly effective group. It means that everyone in the group is able to *live with* and *support* the decision at hand. The move to modified consensus can come at any time during a discussion, as long as all concerns have been identified and addressed to the point at which everyone is comfortable. Reaching modified consensus is attainable in most groups and worth the effort.

The first step in consensus building is to sort out what is worth talking about and what is not. When an issue is being discussed, it makes little sense to dwell on aspects that everyone agrees upon. Once the points of agreement have been identified, they need not be repeated. Yet, it seems to happen often.

Three applicants were being considered for the IT department manager position in a professional services firm. Members of the firm's 12-member operating committee interviewed each of the candidates separately or in teams. The managing partner called a meeting with the entire committee to discuss the pros and cons of each candidate. Although all three looked promising on paper, one candidate did not make an impressive showing in the interviews.

After the interviews, the board met. Someone suggested that members go around in turn and share their thoughts. Jerry was the first person to speak. He said that candidate number three was clearly weaker than the other two, and gave his reasons for this opinion. He said candidates one and two both seemed capable, for different reasons, and it would be difficult to decide on which one would be the best.

Cassandra spoke next. She spent several minutes stating why she thought candidate number three was the weakest of the three, and less time reflecting on her impressions of candidates one and two. Harry was next. You can probably guess where this is going—Harry was adamant in his distain for candidate three, and went on and on.

Jason interrupted Harry, and asked the operating committee members, "Is there anyone around the table who thinks that candidate three is a viable contender for the position?" No one raised a hand or spoke up. Then Jason suggested that they simply focus the remaining discussion on candidates one and two, because everyone agreed that candidate three was not a good fit for the position. Don't waste time in your meetings discussing things on which everyone agrees!

How does a group reach modified consensus anyway? More than most meeting skills, building consensus in a meeting seems to be one of the least understood processes. It doesn't have to be. In fact, consensus decisions flow naturally from practicing the skills regarding planning and flow in parts one and two of this book. Consensus building is a process that evolves naturally in a collaborative meeting. Here are some of the ways to build modified consensus in a collaborative meeting:

> ⇨ Encourage every participant to fully contribute (see Chapters 6 and 7). This means creating an environment in which group members feel safe in offering opinions, ideas, and thought-starters that may not fully developed, and are invited to build on others' contributions.

> ⇨ Summarize frequently (see Chapters 5 and 6). The facilitator or other group members take time out to recap the group's progress, identify or confirm areas of agreement, and isolate areas for further discussion and problem-solving.

> ⇨ Seek to understand everyone's perspective on issues, and then strive for a solution that incorporates the best thinking, yet goes beyond anyone's separate visions of what is possible.

> ⇨ When addressing areas of concern, encourage group members to voice their uneasiness, no matter how slight or

intense, without fear of attack from other group members. The balanced response technique detailed in Chapter 7 is a powerful tool to use for this. Encourage the group to use "How to" and "I wish" language to voice concerns.

⇨ Take a straw vote often to see where the group stands on an issue. The "fist to five" technique that follows is one tool that can be used for this purpose.

⇨ Work on the concerns and areas of disagreement until it becomes apparent that group members agree they have arrived at an acceptable solution, representing the best thinking of the group.

The language to test consensus

It is the facilitator's job to recognize when the group is closing in on a solution or recommendation, and to check out his or her conclusion with the group. Here are examples of language to test consensus:

"Let's see where we stand on (issue). I think we all agree on (XYZ). Do we have everyone's input? Are there any more concerns?"

"How are we doing on this? Is there anything in (the proposal or solution) that is still troublesome?"

"Let's take a straw vote here to get a sense of how close we are to a solution. Are you feeling pretty comfortable with what we are recommending?" A straw vote is very informal. You don't even have to raise hands; just look for "head nods" of agreement, and probe group members whose body language lets you know there may be concerns.

"I am sensing we are in general agreement…who's got any outstanding concerns?"

"Unless there are concerns we need to address, let's move forward…"

"Let's check out how close we are to a solution."

When most participants appear to be comfortable with the proposal or decision, then it is time to ask two key questions:

Consensus

"Can everyone live with and support (the decision/proposal)?"

"Is there anyone who can't live with or support (the decision)?"

Asking the "live with and support" questions in both the positive and the negative invites people to think through their level of comfort and commits them to support the group's decision. Undoubtedly, some will disagree with minor points, but if their concerns have been heard, and honest attempts have been made to address them, they will likely be able to live with and support the decision. Once you have achieved modified consensus, write it down, then move on to other issues.

An important distinction: modified consensus does not mean compromise. The idea of compromise means that someone gives up something important in order to reach an agreement. When a group works through issues to modified consensus, no one has to "give up" anything.

The dynamics of consensus building embrace everything *Make Meetings Matter* is all about: meeting on purpose, good planning, having the right people, focus, facilitation, feedback, and fun. Group consensus is the natural outcome if everything else works. It requires group members to honestly express opinions and concerns, and to be open to suggestions and ideas for addressing them. Consensus also requires an attentive facilitator to know when to "test the waters" and call for closure on an issue or solution.

The "fist to five" straw vote technique

One of my clients, Rajeev Bal of Assurant Health, introduced me to the "fist to five" technique, and I have found it to be a quick and useful method to obtain a straw vote on any issue or decision that a group is considering.

Here's how it works. The facilitator invites participants to raise one hand and hold up anywhere from zero (fist) to five fingers to indicate where they stand on a decision or issue, or their level of agreement. Zero is the lowest rating and five is the highest rating (totally agree and support).

This gives an instant reading on where everybody stands, with degrees of difference. The discussion can then turn to addressing the concerns of those indicating zero to two fingers, turning next to the "three's" while making sure the people showing four to five fingers remain supportive. Indeed, they may be able to convince others of their reasoning.

If nearly everyone is showing three or fewer fingers, the idea or decision probably doesn't have a chance. When everyone is showing four or five, then it's time to ask the "live with and support" questions and declare modified consensus.

Avoid Groupthink

Beware of "groupthink" when attempting to build consensus. Groupthink usually happens when one or a few vocal members are highly persuasive or assertive in pushing for their ideas and points of view, making it somewhat intimidating for less expressive people to voice concerns. As a result, they may "cave in" and go along with the group, even when they have concerns.

Groupthink can also happen when group members are insulated from the realities of the organization, such as boards or executive committees who are not in touch with what is happening at the operating level. They may be unaware of their blindsides. The "emperor's new clothes" version of groupthink is reinforced when underlings are too intimidated to question the boss' decision or point out its flaws.

Originally labeled by psychologist Irving L. Janis, groupthink can also happen in groups that have been meeting throughout a period of time without entertaining diverse viewpoints. Long meetings may also produce "same old" groupthink; everyone wants to go home, so decisions may be rushed. Similarly, when groups are under pressure to make a decision, members may bypass their usual assessment criteria, for the sake of group harmony. The risk of groupthink is that less than optimum solutions are reached because of the lack of critical evaluation—all points of view are not heard.

Consensus

To avoid groupthink, give consideration to the following:

⇨ Welcome diversity in your group. Invite people from other departments, people who are known to have different viewpoints from your own, and people who will be affected by the decisions your group will make.

⇨ The initiator (boss, committee head) sets the tone for divergent viewpoints. Participants must feel safe in expressing their reservations, instead of just saying what the boss wants to hear. A group that has no conflict may fall victim to groupthink.

⇨ If the group reaches a decision too quickly or without vigorous discussion, consider delaying making it until everyone has a chance to think it over. This might also allow time for more research or data gathering to support the decision.

⇨ Seek the opinions of others in the organization before making a final decision. Tell them what you are considering, and why you think it will work. Listen carefully for input and suggestions to make your proposal stronger.

RIGHT PEOPLE/CLEAR LEVEL OF AUTHORITY

There are few things more demoralizing than to have a higher-up shoot down a group's decision after the meeting. Of course, senior executives and managers always reserve the prerogative to make final decisions. The trouble comes when the group is told they are empowered to decide (or thinks they are), when in fact that is not the case.

If the senior person has a strong point of view on an issue, then he or she is obligated to share that with the group, preferably by showing up at the meeting and fully participating. If you initiate a meeting to get ideas or feedback from people, it is important to be very clear about your intentions.

Let participants know how their ideas and recommendations be processed and used—how, when, and by whom decisions will be made and action taken. Without this clarity, the whole process may backfire.

It may not be necessary or practical for the senior person to attend the entire meeting. Indeed, in some cases, the boss's presence may stifle thinking. One solution is for the boss to show up at the beginning of an idea-generation session to set the tone, clarify the goals, and share any thoughts he or she may have. Once the group has done its work, the boss attends the wrap-up to hear their recommendations, thrash out any concerns, and give her or her approval. Using this approach ensures the boss's input is considered, and has the potential of getting the best thinking out of the group. Group members' level of commitment to the ultimate course of action is also likely to be extremely high.

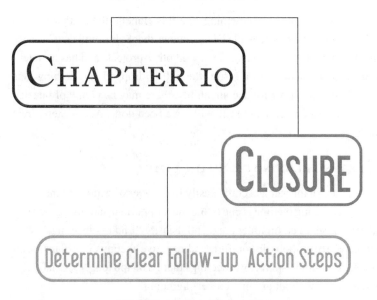

CHAPTER 10

CLOSURE

Determine Clear Follow-up Action Steps

The Truth You Never Hear

"Well, we've stumbled along for more than three hours, and we're almost done with the agenda. I hope somebody picks up the ball on all this stuff, because there's a lot to do if we're going to meet our deadlines. I wonder what should we do with the items we weren't able to cover...maybe they will just go away."

The Challenges

No Action/Fuzzy Action Steps

Most decisions made in a meeting are not an end—rather they are part of a process of getting something done, solving problems, and developing and implementing a plan. Decisions require action: somebody must to do something as a result. The action may be relatively easy, such as notifying other people, or more complex such as initiating a research project. When actions steps are not clearly spelled out, problems inevitably occur.

The scene may go something like this: Janelle thinks that Dick is going to write the report, while Dick assumes that Sylvia will do it because she wrote the last one. Sylvia is busy on other projects and has no intention of taking action. As a result, the ball is dropped and nothing gets done. When it is time for accountability, there may be plenty of puzzled looks ("I assumed...") and little will have been done. Action steps are a must.

Meetings Do Not End on Time

Although this subject could easily fit in several sections of the book, ending a meeting on time is one of the most important actions a group can take to preserve commitment and enthusiasm. "Endless meetings" are a source of frustration, discomfort, and negative feelings in groups of all kinds. Few people appreciate meetings that go on too long, especially if it just happens without group members agreeing.

Leaders who allow meetings to go overtime without renegotiation make an implicit assumption that group members have nothing better to do with their time than to stay in the meeting. This ignores the fact that most people would rather speak for themselves regarding their time commitments. A scheduled one-hour meeting is not a license to hold people captive all morning or afternoon!

My experience, confirmed by informal research, indicates that lengthy meetings are a major frustration for people in organizations of all kinds. Many people have told me that long drawn-out meetings are a primary reason they do not volunteer for committees, boards, and task groups. The problem can undermine the ability of the group to function. In business organizations, although people may not have a choice of whether or not to be in a meeting, their time is valuable. Spending long hours in meetings may not be the best use of it.

Strategies and Solutions for Closure and Clarity

⇨ Assign specific action steps before the meeting ends: what will be done, by whom, and when. Agree on follow-up.

⇨ End the meeting on time, or renegotiate the time contract with participants.

ASSIGN SPECIFIC ACTION STEPS

Most decisions set things in motion, and are not an end unto themselves. Action is required. Action steps have three components: what, who, and when.

The "what" should be very specific, so that there will be no misunderstanding by any group member or recipient regarding the action to be taken. Examples:

⇨ Conduct additional research among key customer segments.

⇨ Prepare presentation for executive team.

⇨ Write proposal to request funds.

⇨ Write job descriptions for analyst position.

⇨ Establish specifications for project RFP.

Who will do it? Assign specific responsibility for all action steps. This means asking for volunteers or assigning the action steps to individuals who agree to complete it by the time indicated.

When must it be done? This simply means laying out the target dates for completion of the action, or at least the next step. It is useful to establish checkpoints or milestones so that there are no surprises on the due date.

Examples of action steps, incorporating what, who, and when:

What will be done	Who will do it	By when
Write proposal requesting additional consumer research	Joan	March 3
Review proposal and forward	Ed	March 6
Evaluate group's ideas for new vendor guidelines	Johanna, Susan, Eric	March 12
Make minimum of six calls to members for capital campaign	All committee members	Complete by March 24
Select vendors to make proposals for integrated phone and computer system	John, Vance, Tim	March 20
Develop engineering drawings for fuel transport system and forward to Elson	Neil, Jennifer (+ Eldon review)	March 20–submit March 25–approve

As action items come up during the meeting, it's a good idea to capture them and note them in some special way. For example, assign the recorder or someone else to write action steps on a separate piece of paper or flip chart sheet. Consultant Mike Scott recommends action steps be captured on a different colored piece of paper, so they are clearly recognizable by all. If you are using a computer, simply highlight action items or capture them in a separate section of the notes. Toward the end of the meeting, the recorder or facilitator reviews all action items, and makes sure that everyone agrees.

Many groups get stuck on the "who" part of action items. I have observed that some people may be reluctant to bring up ideas, because they think they will get saddled with doing the work. This shouldn't be surprising, because some people are better at generating ideas, whereas others are more adept at follow-through and implementation. In fact, you could be inviting disappointment if you give a good "generator" the responsibility for detailed follow-through. When a meeting is focused on idea-generation, the person(s) best suited for action and follow-through might not be obvious. Solution? Make it clear at the outset that both skills (idea generation and action/follow-through) are critical, and that being an idea generator does not mean you will be the project implementer. At the end of the idea generation or in a follow-up meeting, ask people to volunteer for the steps or identify others who are capable and willing to take on the next phase.

As will be noted in Chapter 12, one of the most important parts of the meeting summary is the recap of actions.

END MEETINGS ON TIME

Most group members are all smiles when a productive meeting ends on time, and they are often astonished when it ends early! Impossible dream? If you have followed the recommendations for planning, flow, and completion in this book, you are likely to manage your meetings so that they end as scheduled or earlier, with a sense of accomplishment. As you have no doubt figured out, it takes careful preparation, active facilitation, and accurate assignment of follow-up steps to make this happen.

A clear purpose, prioritized agenda, and the right people are the starting points. Having an effective facilitator to manage the discussions and keep things on track is a must. Still, you will undoubtedly reach the target ending time of many meetings and still have unfinished business. There may be important items left in the parking lot. Maybe everyone realized that more analysis was needed on an issue to make an informed decision. Perhaps it took a lot longer than anyone realized to reach modified consensus on an important recommendation. Whatever the reason, the time comes, and there is a decision to be made. Do you just end the meeting, or keep going?

Hopefully, your meetings won't reach this point, because you have been monitoring time throughout, so that you know exactly where you are and what you have left to do. In longer meetings, you have revisited your agenda to make mid-course corrections that will still enable the group to achieve the purpose and end on time. Some discussion items have been dropped or compressed, others have been expanded.

As noted in Chapter 4, a functional agenda always includes some time at the end to wrap up loose ends, usually the last 10 or 15 minutes. As you will see in Chapter 12, taking a few minutes to evaluate the effectiveness of your meeting is always useful. The initiator or facilitator should use that time to briefly summarize what the group has accomplished, revisit parking lot items and decide what to do with them, review key decisions and action steps, do a +/△ on the meeting, and thank the group. Administrative items, such as confirming the next meeting date, time, and place are often the very last things to cover. Who is responsible for bringing closure and ending on time? Ultimately, this is the facilitator's responsibility, with the agreement of the initiator and group members.

Renegotiating the time contract

If you are close to the end of the agreed-on meeting time, and it is clear some important issues will not be finished, one of the *least* effective things you can do when time is up is to simply forge ahead without comment. Although it may be tempting, this does not respect participants' valuable time, regardless of their relationship to the group or the initiator. A better alternative is for the facilitator, with the agreement of the initiator, to renegotiate the time contract with group members. This can be a succinct request, such as: "It seems important to get everyone's input on this before tomorrow's management conference. Is everybody okay with extending the meeting another 15 minutes?" On some occasions, extending a meeting (or portion of a meeting that is part of a longer conference or retreat) can be produce great results. If the group is "on a roll," the extended time can create a sense of urgency to focus toward completion. However, I recommend that extending meetings, even with the agreement of all members, should be the exception rather than the rule, and should be done sparingly.

Bringing on-time closure to a productive meeting that has achieved its purpose is one of the sweetest rewards for good planning, time management, and facilitation.

CHAPTER 11

CRITIQUE AND CELEBRATION

Evaluate Group Effectiveness

The Truth You'd Love to Hear, Just Once

"Nathan, you were incredibly obnoxious and overbearing in our meeting today. Not only did you ramble off in a hundred different directions, you used your sick humor to offend several people. Furthermore, you managed to interrupt just about everybody. Now, for the rest of you..."

The Challenges

NOT ASSESSING MEETING OR GROUP EFFECTIVENESS

You had a great meeting. Energy was high, the focus was clear, and many breakthrough ideas were generated. Differing points of view were aired, and the group reached modified consensus decisions on the key issues. Clear action steps were assigned. The meeting started and ended on time. Everyone attending agreed it was one of the best meetings they had ever attended.

Two weeks later the same group of people met to focus on additional challenges facing the organization. Things were different from the very beginning, however. The energy level was lower. Several group members launched into tangents and "rabbit holes" that resulted in the meeting straying off track several times. A few people shut down and did not contribute much. The hardest part was trying to decide on a course of action. The meeting ran overtime, with many loose ends unresolved. Everyone agreed it was one of the worst meetings they had ever attended.

What made the first meeting work so well and the second meeting with the same group fail so miserably? Without any more information than is given, it is hard to tell. The problem with both meetings is that the group did not spend any time assessing what worked well and what could be improved. Without this critical appraisal, group members will never really know how to make—or keep—meetings more effective, except by chance.

Individual or Group Contributions Go Unrecognized

Normally, Roxanne was quiet in committee meetings. In the March meeting, however, things were different. It was clear that Roxanne had spent extra time and energy to gather input on how to get more volunteers for the group's major fundraising effort. She had done extra research on the Internet and consulted several experts, and consequently her ideas were fresh, strategically sound, and well thought out.

Unfortunately, several important items were on the committee's agenda for the March meeting. As a result, when Roxanne offered her ideas, her extra efforts went unrecognized. The fundraising program seemed to be lost in the myriad of other issues discussed by the group, including a heated discussion on the budget. The group did not process her ideas and recommendations, and no one acknowledged Roxanne for her extra efforts. As you might expect, for the next few meetings, Roxanne retreated to her "quiet mode" once again, and contributed only minimally to the topics under discussion.

Some meetings are so task oriented and serious that they concentrate solely on the work at hand. Many initiators and facilitators fail to appreciate the power of positive recognition and affirmation.

Strategies and Solutions
for Evaluating Meetings and Recognizing People

⇨ Take time to do a +/△(plus/delta) debrief after each meeting, identifying what worked and what could be changed or improved.

⇨ Consider using a process observer.

⇨ Recognize individual and group contributions.

⇨ Celebrate success after a particularly productive or energizing meeting.

PLUS/DELTA (+/△) DEBRIEF

It is highly productive to take a few minutes at the end of every meeting to identify:

Pluses (+). List the major things that happened in the meeting that worked. This includes identifying techniques used by group members or the facilitator to stay on task or build group cohesiveness, recognizing presentations that were succinct and informative or acknowledging individual contributions. These are the things that the group wants to maintain and build upon.

Deltas ($\triangle$). Include on this list things that can be changed or done differently to improve effectiveness at the next meeting. This might include observations on counter-productive discussions, disruptive behaviors, poor time management, or other things that derailed the meeting. An important part of this discussion is to solicit suggestions on what might be done differently next time.

Once a group gets the hang of it, a +/$\triangle$can be done in a few minutes. Beware of over-generalizing. There is a tendency to think that everything went well in an effective meeting, and that everything went wrong in a meeting that is generally boring or non-productive. The reality is that in every meeting, some things work and some things do not.

At the end of a recent planning conference, Melissa, the facilitator, drew a vertical line down the middle of a flip chart, making two columns. She put a plus sign at the top of the left column and drew a triangle at the top of the right column. Melissa then asked participants to imagine that the entire meeting had been recorded on video, and that they were able to play back highlights of the meeting in their mind. This imaginary video was set to pause every time there was something that was really positive about the meeting—things that helped it succeed, made it fun, or moved the meeting along. It would also pause, she explained, at points when things happened that you might want to change if you had the chance—things that bogged down the meeting, threw it off-track, or were unproductive.

After a minute or so of the reflection, she invited people to come up to the flip chart, and to write the "good stuff" in the + column, and to list things they would like to see done differently or changed at the next meeting in the $\triangle$column. Melissa encouraged every group member to contribute at least one item to each list, putting a check mark by items that duplicated their thoughts.

Critique and Celebration

Here are some of the responses:

+ (Things That Worked)	△(What Could We Improve)
Generated lots of good ideas; built on each other's ideas ✓✓✓	Start the meeting on time, without waiting for late-comers ✓
Had agenda in advance, with a chance to update at beginning	Limit discussion on items so everyone gets a chance to comment✓✓✓✓
Stuck to agenda pretty well✓✓	Come better prepared
Summarized results and action steps at the end	Establish a ground rule for side conversations

She then asked for comments; the interchange was both lively and informative. The group then committed to remember and reinforce the pluses, and work on ways to address the deltas. At the next planning session, the list was reviewed, and specific ideas were implemented for suggested improvements.

Critiquing a meeting in this way provides guidance for initiators, facilitators, and participants. Using a +/△list, which is similar to the balanced response technique described in Chapter 7, reinforces positive skills and behaviors, and clarifies things that can be improved to make the group's meetings more effective. While it is best to debrief the meeting at the very end, you can also ask for a +/△via e-mail or electronic questionnaire.

For groups that meet frequently, such as committees, staff groups, and teams, a more comprehensive +/△evaluation is useful from time to time. Have each meeting participant fill out an evaluation, and summarize the results for distribution to all. See the sample form in the Appendix.

Process Observer

When participants are in the midst of a lively meeting, it isn't always apparent to them what is happening to enhance or detract from the meeting's effectiveness. For this reason, it is often useful to appoint a process observer: someone who is charged with monitoring behaviors and skills that contribute to and take away from the meeting's success. Generally, the process observer does not participate in the subject of the meeting, but is there simply to monitor the meeting and provide feedback.

At the end of the meeting, the process observer may give a +/△report to the facilitator, initiator, or the group on what was observed. By rotating this task, each participant will become more aware of meeting process skills, and in turn, become better meeting participants.

Recognize Individual Contributions

Meeting initiators, facilitators, and group members who take the time to recognize individual and group efforts are paving the way for enthusiastic participation and more effective meetings. Psychologists understand that behavior that is rewarded gets repeated—the more people are recognized for things they do to improve meetings the more likely they are to repeat these positive behaviors. This can be especially beneficial in groups that are just learning about the skills for running effective meetings. Recognitions and celebrations do not have to be long and drawn-out; a simple observation can often work just as well. Examples:

"Elysse, your research was very helpful to our understanding of the extent of the problem. You did a great job of summarizing it for us."

"Bill, when you suggested we all go around and give our opinions of the new personnel policy, it really helped us focus and get everyone's point of view."

"When Allen told us how his people tried to implement the new voicemail system, I thought I would die laughing. Allen, your humor really helped us all understand the work we have to do."

Critique and Celebration

"Rosita's observation that we were all too close to the situation to be objective was right on target. After we gather some customer comments, we will be in a better position to understand how our system really works. Thanks, Rosita."

Spontaneous applause for individuals, breakout teams, or the entire group is a powerful way to show appreciation. All it takes is for one person (the facilitator or anyone else) to start, and the rest of the group will join in. Think of a time when you were applauded for something you did. How did it make you feel? You can give that same gift to anyone who deserves it. If you are meeting via teleconference and want to "applaud" someone, have each participant press the 3 key (or any other numeric key). In Internet-supported collaborative meetings, emoticons (electronic "attaboys") can be transmitted to recognize positive contributions.

Sandy wasn't the most talkative person in the problem-solving meeting. While always cordial, she tended to listen intently, but seldom spoke. Many in the group thought she wasn't really engaged in the topic because of her silence. After an intense discussion on alternatives for solving the problem at hand—a glitch in the process for handling customer complaints—Sandy spoke up. She suggested an elegant solution to centralize the process rather than having each division deal with complaints individually.

Several group members were surprised at how they had all missed the "obvious" solution, and broke out into spontaneous applause for Sandy's clear thinking. After that meeting, no one was bothered by Sandy's silence during meetings. In fact, the group often called on her toward the end of a discussion to elicit her feedback and ideas. When Sandy spoke, they listened!

Positive feedback can be made anytime during the meeting. Encourage participants to identify and bring up positive contributions as they occur, and again at the end of the meeting.

CELEBRATE SUCCESS AFTER
PRODUCTIVE OR ENERGIZING MEETINGS

After a particularly productive meeting, why not do something special to celebrate? Here are some suggestions:

⇨ Order pizza (or other food) and beverages at the end of the meeting, and celebrate with an instant party.

⇨ Do an "instant replay" of something funny or interesting that occurred in the meeting.

⇨ Present mock awards to participants, such as "best idea generator," "most intense," or "world's best recorder."

⇨ Go out for food with the group. It can simply be a get-together with snacks and beverages, or a more elaborate dinner. Such an outing will also allow group members the opportunity to get to know one another better in a relaxed setting.

⇨ During longer planning sessions and retreats, consider cutting one or more scheduled work sessions short as a reward for productive work early on. This could be set up at the beginning of the conference; for example, let the group know that you will eliminate one afternoon work session if the group is able to accomplish certain goals in the early sessions. This can be free time for participants, or scheduled activities such as golf or tennis, spa visits, or hikes.

⇨ As the initiator, write every participant a personal note as a "thank you" for his or her contribution to a great meeting.

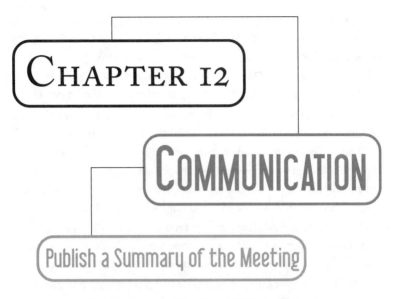

CHAPTER 12

COMMUNICATION

Publish a Summary of the Meeting

The Statement You Hear All Too Often

"Francis, did you second the motion to authorize funds to repair the water fountain, or was it Virginia? And who was it that suggested that we meet every other week during the summer months? Was that made into a motion? Let me read the exact wording back to you to make sure it is right."

The Challenges

No Record of the Meeting Is Kept

Many groups, especially those that meet together often, neither keep nor publish any record of their meetings. This is fine for some groups, such as social or study groups. For task-oriented groups, however, this can cause problems, especially when somebody drops the ball. In my experience, having no record of the meeting works only if each person is disciplined to record his or her action steps, and there is a high trust and accountability level among group members. For many of us, however, if things are not written down, we tend to forget (or selectively remember) commitments, action steps, and timetables. Worse, good ideas that are not recorded and published may be lost forever. I have also observed groups where someone, usually the secretary or recorder, takes notes, but then does not distribute a summary to group members. What's the point?

Several years ago, I was a member on the publicity committee for a community theater group. On this committee, I was a participant, not the facilitator. The group was composed of highly knowledgeable and creative people, and at one meeting we batted around dozens of ideas for getting the word out about the upcoming theater season. Some ideas had great potential, others were outrageous, and still others were so-so. There were six people attending, and no one recorded the ideas. At the end of an hour, two members had to leave. There was no feedback about the ideas, nor was any attempt made to summarize and decide the best ideas.

Marian, the committee chair, thanked everybody and said she would take care of the publicity for the next season. When the publicity program was implemented, it seemed to miss the mark. Worse, the group had generated ideas that would have solved some of the problems we were experiencing. It seemed as if Mary did not value our input, or maybe she just missed the ideas we had generated. If a summary of the ideas had been prepared and sent to the committee members, others working on the program might have been able to rescue the plan.

MEETING SUMMARIES ARE NEEDLESSLY DETAILED

The exactness and perfection of the group's secretary nearly drove the other group members crazy. Virtually every phrase uttered in the meeting was captured, and certainly every motion was rendered in precise language, including who made it, who seconded it, and how many voted yea or nay, often by name. In fact, the secretary interrupted the meeting flow several times to clarify things that were said and who said them.

It was difficult to trudge through the published minutes, because everything that happened was there, in exacting detail. Because of the length and detail of the minutes, group members seldom took the time to read through them, and those who did often missed important items. For example, many action steps were missed, because they were buried so deeply in the information. At the beginning of each meeting, the chair called for the minutes from the previous meeting to be approved; this process often took several minutes and started the meeting off in "low gear." In fact, few people had even read the minutes before the meeting, because they were so lengthy and "dense." In a court of law or in the halls of congress, verbatim minutes are necessary. For the rest of us, a better alternative is called for.

ASSUMING THINGS WILL HAPPEN WITHOUT REMINDERS

We would love to think that our memories are perfect, and that our priorities are always in sync so that we always finish the most important things first. In this ideal state, we would follow up on projects and work assignments in a timely fashion. We would be totally prepared for each meeting we attend and ready to report on items for which we are responsible. Does this sound like utopia? Unfortunately, it probably is for most people. We are human. Our lives are filled to overflowing with dozens of priorities related to work, family, friends, clubs, church, and recreation.

It is not prudent to assume that because someone takes responsibility for an action item, and receives a reminder in the meeting summary, that it will get done. How many times have you been disappointed to learn that a project you understood would be completed hadn't even been started? Although lack of follow-through can be critical in businesses, it is also a problem in organizations and boards that depend on volunteers to get the work done. The time to solve follow-through problems is before the next meeting.

Strategies and Solutions
for Clear Communications and Follow-Through

⇨ Using the group notes as a guide, prepare a concise written summary of major discussion items, action steps, timetables, and people responsible.

⇨ Send the summary to all attendees—and others who need to know—as soon as possible following the meeting via e-mail.

⇨ Establish a ground rule for accountability in your group.

⇨ Initiate a follow-up system to periodically check on the progress of projects and timetables.

Prepare a Concise Summary

Group notes are a powerful technique for posting the agenda, recording ideas, noting decisions made, and tracking action steps during the meeting. The most effective way to do this is for the recorder to keep track of these items on a flip chart or computer, preferably with a display projector. This enables all group members to see the output in "real time." Although group notes are valuable during the meeting to keep focused, they also provide the raw material for writing a meeting summary.

The summary should include:

1. A recap of the main discussions.

2. Decisions made.

3. Action steps: what will be done, by whom and when.

4. Meeting process debrief.

The operative word is *concise*. An ideal meeting summary should be as brief as possible, no more than one or two pages long. Meeting summary templates are available in the Appendix. Here are two sample minutes/summaries:

Communication

Meeting Summary

Company/Organization:	General Manufacturing
Department/Team/Committee:	Benefits Task Force
Meeting Initiator:	Suzie Martin
Date/Time:	October 15, 2008, 9:05–10:15 a.m.
Meeting Location:	Main Conference Room
Meeting Purpose:	Review policies for 401K, vacation, and stock purchase plan. Generate ideas for additional benefits.
Facilitator & Recorder:	Lenny Baxter, Nina Hotchkiss
Copy to Participants Plus:	Todd Adams

Participants:	
Caitlin Armstrong	Grace Vanders
Jennifer Stansted	Marvin Woolford

Meeting Minutes & Action Summary

Agenda Item: Vacation Policy

Presenter or Discussion Leader: Caitlin

Key Conclusions/Summary of Discussion and Decisions:

- Agreed that individual contributors could direct their plan
  funds into an expanded list of alternative investments.

Action Items

What will be done	Who will do it	By when
Investigate alternatives with broker (Rausch)	Marvin	Next meeting

Agenda Item: Vacation Policy

Presenter or Discussion Leader: Grace

Key Conclusions/Summary of Discussion & Decisions:

- Employee survey strongly supported floating holiday concept. Agreed to offer it beginning March 1 to all employees.

- Results of informal survey of four local companies showed our current policy (one week vacation after one year's employment) was out of line. Group agreed to recommend modifying policy to one week vacation after six months, two weeks after one year.

Action Items

What will be done	Who will do it	By when
Prepare announcement	Grace and Jennifer	Nov. 15
Prepare recommendation and present to Operating Committee	Grace	December meeting (review 1 week prior)

Agenda Item: Stock Purchase Plan

Presenter or Discussion Leader: Nina

Key Conclusions/Summary of Discussion & Decisions:

- Agreed to allow any employee to purchase shares of company stock with no commission.

- Discussed brochure and agreed that participants need to be informed about short-term market fluctuations and risks.

Action Items

What will be done	Who will do it	By when
Get Treasurer (Bob) to sign off	Nina	Nov. 8
Incorporate "risk" language in brochure	Jennifer	January reprint

Communication

Agenda Item: Brainstorming—additional ideas

Presenter or Discussion Leader: Lenny

Ideas that group felt had merit for further development:

- Offer financial planning as a benefit—no cost to employees with five-plus years, and for new hires at department head and higher level.

- Mentoring program: each employee would have senior mentor (not boss) for first two years.

- Convert the old garage into a fitness center, open to all employees.

- Offer training in general communications skills: writing, speaking, and running meetings.

Action Items

What will be done	Who will do it	By when
Flesh out ideas and project costs	Suzie	Nov. 15

Parking Lot Items

- Allow employees to take their birthday as a holiday—handled by new floating holiday policy.

- Personalized mugs for break area—no action now.

Meeting Debrief

Plusses

- Everyone attended, only one person late.

- Materials handed out in advance for discussion items.

- Lenny's first try at facilitating was terrific.

Deltas

- Started five minutes late—let's try to all honor start time.

- A couple of side conversations got us off track (thanks, Nina for get us back on agenda!).

- Need to allow more time to cover parking lot items.

Next Meeting: December 11 at 9 a.m.—Room to be announced.

Facilitator: Nina

Meeting Minutes

Company/Organization:	First Church
Department/Team/Committee:	Board
Meeting Initiator:	Rev. F. Durkee
Date/Time:	June 16, 2008, 6:40–8:00 p.m.
Meeting Location:	Library
Meeting Purpose:	Monthly meeting to receive updates on committee projects
Facilitator & Recorder:	L. Herbert, C. Davis
Copy to Participants Plus:	Permanent file

Attending:		
D. Crandall	C. Harris	L. Herbert (Chair)
K. Normal	P. MacIvers	H. Pancero
F. Wilder	C. Davis (recorder)	

Meeting Minutes & Action Summary

Discussions and Decisions:

- Building/Grounds: staining of church entrance and tile work two weeks behind schedule; does not affect overall renovation completion date of September 1.

- Pastoral Care: approved ideas for contacting lapsed members.

- Education: education committee's +/△ on spring program was discussed (see separate attachment). All agreed better and earlier publicity should result in higher fall attendance.

- Finance: see separate summary of financial reports. Refinance of mortgage of education building will save $575 per month in operating budget.

- Senior pastor: Recommended all-church dinner to replace annual meeting in early 2009. Goal: to enable people who attend different services to get to know each other, and to celebrate the completion of the renovation project. Board approved.

Action Items

What will be done	Who will do it	By when
Church workday plan	K. Normal	July 15
Recruit volunteers for workday	H. Pancero	July 1–15
Set schedule for follow up on lapsed members	P. MacIvers	August 8
Fall program to be "previewed" in bulletin starting in July, with details mid-August	K. Wilder	Per schedule
Develop plans for all-church dinner	D. Crandall	October 6

Parking Lot Items

- Bylaws revision: agreed to appoint committee for review at July meeting.

Meeting Debrief:

Plusses

- Ended on time, despite 10 minute late start.

- Great ideas generated for lapsed member initiative.

Deltas

- Bylaws discussion took too much time—agree to put in parking lot earlier.

Next Meeting: Monday, July 28. Review bylaws before meeting.

As seen in the examples, all action steps are highlighted in a separate section that includes a brief statement of what will be done, who will do it, and when. As a further reinforcement and reminder, the recorder (or whomever sends out the summary) can highlight each member's copy with action steps and follow-up for that person marked with a highlighter pen.

If your group has difficulty weaning away from highly detailed minutes, take a look at minutes or summaries from several previous meetings. How important or useful are explicit notes about who said what, who made and seconded motions, and so on? How is such information used? How does it serve the purpose of the group? If the only answer to any of these questions is "We've always done it that way," or "It's in our bylaws," consider changing the procedure, the bylaws, or both, and move to preparing concise meeting summaries similar to the previous examples.

Send the Summary to People Who Need to Know

Preparing a summary will not accomplish much if participants and others do not receive it in a timely manner. Once it is completed, the meeting summary should be sent to:

⇨ People who attended the meeting, highlighting action steps on individual copies.

⇨ Group members and other interested people who did not attend the meeting.

The summary should be sent as soon as possible after the meeting, ideally within 24 hours. This will remind people of action steps while the "news" is still fresh, and allow any incorrect information to be changed if required.

If the meeting summary is delayed, it may get lost in the clutter of other priorities, or with the notes of three other meetings people have attended since yours.

You may want to send the meeting summary to one or two attendees to check for accuracy prior to sending it out to everyone. Once the recorder (or other person designated) sends out the meeting summary, it is then the responsibility of all recipients to read it thoroughly, and to take action on items for which they are responsible.

One of the great time-wasters is to hand out the previous meeting's summary at the beginning of the next meeting. By then, it may be too late to take action, and "reviewing the minutes" will consume valuable meeting time.

Establish a Ground Rule for Accountability

When groups are first forming and members are trying to figure out their level of commitment and involvement, it is useful to establish and enforce ground rules for accountability. In its simplest form, accountability means that group members commit to doing what they say they will do, when they say they will do it.

In ongoing groups, if there is no problem with follow-through, you may not need to address this issue. However, if some members are weak in follow-through on action items, accountability should be addressed as a group standard to which all members agree. The process of affirming a ground rule of this type with other group members serves to remind everyone that commitments are taken seriously.

Implement a Follow-up System

A follow-up system for action items is like an insurance policy. It will help insure that actions are taken and projects stay on track. Depending on the group, the person responsible for follow-up can be the initiator, facilitator, or recorder. Follow-up may also be delegated to someone else, such as an administrative assistant. Follow-up communications needn't be heavy-handed; often a quick reminder is all that is needed. It is better to initiate a quick e-mail or phone call on Wednesday to remind someone of the report due at Friday's meeting, than to arrive at the meeting on Friday and be surprised or disappointed.

On more complex projects, it's a good idea for the group or project leader to get more involved by checking with people frequently between meetings, and offering help if needed. The following are some follow-up options to consider:

Send a reminder by e-mail

"Edwina, a reminder that your analysis of survey results is due at our next staff meeting. Let me know if you need any assistance in completing this."

"Looking forward to your report on membership at the Feb. 12 conference. If you run into any snags in getting it done, Cas said he might be able to lend a hand. Give him or me a call if you need help."

Send out a copy of the meeting summary highlighting the action step(s), perhaps with a hand-written note

"Don, you really wowed us last meeting—thanks for your insightful contributions. We are all excited about your report on Phase 2 next meeting."

Pick up the phone and call the person

"Hi, Carol, this is Josh. Just checking over the notes from last meeting and wanted to see if you needed any help to prepare the budget presentation for next Monday's meeting."

Leave the door open for people to ask for help

In every follow-up communication, allow for the opportunity for people to ask for help if they need it. There may be dozens of legitimate reasons why something is not done or falls behind schedule, and the time to find out about it is before the next meeting. This will give you the ability to respond by giving input or assistance, assigning the project to someone else or doing it yourself. It is more productive to focus on what needs to be done to get or keep something on track than to ask why it is behind schedule.

With a solid follow-up and accountability system, the meeting process comes full circle. Action steps and follow-up are a critical part of the preparation for the group's next meeting.

Recap of Part III

Most meetings are not over when the group leaves the room. Understanding that meetings are held to accomplish specific purposes, the discussions and decisions almost always require action and follow-up of some kind. In addition, the only way for a group to improve its meeting effectiveness is to do a +/△to identify things that worked and things that can be improved. Remember the 4 C's:

1. *Consensus:* Strive for robust discussions and move toward modified consensus, where everyone can live with and support the decisions or course of action.

2. *Closure:* Establish clear action steps, timetables, and responsibilities—who will do what by when. End on time, leaving time for parking lot and other items, or renegotiate with the group to extend.

3. *Critique and Celebration:* Do a +/△to assess the meeting effectiveness and acknowledge the contributions of those who made it work.

4.   *Communication:* Prepare a concise summary including action steps and distribute it as soon as possible after the meeting; establish a follow-up system to keep projects on track.

Taking Your Group's Temperature

The first 12 chapters of *Make Meetings Matter* provide a solid framework for making meetings more effective. You may be already doing many of these things well in the meetings you initiate, facilitate, or attend. Maybe all you need are small refinements. Other areas may need more attention. Perhaps most business meetings you attend are effective, but the volunteer meetings you attend are a disaster.

Awareness is the first step. If you believe there is value in making your meetings matter via these techniques, share the information with other group members in organizations to which you belong. Please remember that awareness alone is only the first step—it takes practice. Start by trying out a few strategies and ideas you think will make a difference. Once your meetings begins to function more effectively when using them, move on to additional techniques.

What if your group members could care less or push back when you try to introduce some strategies and ideas to improve meetings? Is there anything one person can do to make a difference in meetings, even if you are not the facilitator? Fortunately, the answer is yes. For starters, review the skills for effective participation and facilitation in Chapters 5 and 6. Encourage people who bring up ideas; credit them and build ideas to make them stronger. Point out positive behaviors to group members. Suggest a +/△debrief. Your example may prompt questions from other group members, and after they "tug on your sleeve," you can introduce other skills to help your meetings out.

When understood and practiced, the strategies and ideas in this book will go a long way to make your meetings matter. Accept where your group is, and acknowledge what you are doing that works. Build on that to make meetings more effective, incorporating new techniques as the group is ready.

The next section of the book deals with specific techniques for dealing with disruptive behaviors as well as some tips for electronic and one-on-one meetings.

PART IV

ADDITIONAL STRATEGIES AND SOLUTIONS

DISRUPTIVE BEHAVIORS AND HOW TO DEAL THEM

General guidelines and identifying specific behaviors that disrupt meetings and dealing with them.

USING TECHNOLOGY TO ENHANCE MEETINGS

Strategies and techniques for phone conferences, and synchronous and asynchronous computer-assisted meetings.

ONE-ON-ONE MEETINGS

Strategies and techniques for managing scheduled and impromptu one-on-meetings.

" Our studies show staff meetings to be 28% more productive since we got the ejection seat for Mercer."

CHAPTER 13

DISRUPTIVE BEHAVIORS AND HOW TO DEAL WITH THEM

The Truth You'd Love to Hear, Just Once

"Sam, we know you're the boss, but you're driving us crazy. If you interrupt one more time with your meaningless platitudes, you're outta here."

The Challenges

SOME PEOPLE JUST DON'T GET IT

It seems that there is always one person (or more) in meetings who just doesn't get it. They appear to be interested more in their own agenda than the group's purpose, they choose not to play by the ground rules, or maybe they just don't know any better. Perhaps they are just having a bad day. Whatever the reasons, a series of disruptions can drag down a meeting quite rapidly. Often, a few "bombs" dramatically change the course of a meeting, sometimes beyond repair. In such cases, more than first aid may be required. It could be time for intensive care or major surgery.

AN AGGRESSIVE APPROACH MAY BACKFIRE

It seldom works to fight fire with fire when addressing disruptive behaviors in a meeting. For several years, there was a "town hall" meeting in our community. Several board members had prepared some general remarks to set the tone of the meeting, including Jay, who was the mayor. Shortly after Jay began speaking, Sean interrupted him. Sean's voice was loud, and his tone was heated. He attacked the board on everything from policy to minute details of how the library was being run. At first Jay attempted to ignore Sean, which was difficult. Then Jay would say something such as, "Sean, hold on a minute," but still Sean kept interrupting.

It quickly turned into a battle of wills, and Jay started talking louder. Sean demanded answers, such as "What about the cost overruns on the teen center?" and "How come you haven't moved faster on selecting a new waste hauler?" Jay's patience was being tested. Finally, he cracked. He turned to Sean and yelled, "Damn it, Sean! Shut up! I've got the floor and I'd like to finish my remarks."

Sean finally stormed out of the meeting, and Jay was able to finish. Many people sided with Jay, and said that he was right. However, Jay won the battle and lost the war. Sean was a valuable member of the community, who had been active in many areas. Basically, he had the town's best interests in mind, and he probably didn't know any other way to express his frustrations. As a result of Jay's attack on Sean, he gradually withdrew from active participation in most community activities. Nothing Jay said to Sean after that could repair the damage he had done by confronting him publicly.

Addressing disruptive behaviors requires a delicate balance between assertiveness and tact. The immediate goal is to preserve the integrity of the meeting and not to claim a victory over the person or people who are causing the problem. A longer-term goal is to do what is possible to prevent behaviors from happening over and over.

Strategies and Solutions for Handling Disruptive Behaviors

⇨ Focus on the behavior rather than the person during the meeting.

⇨ Invoke ground rules as the "neutral judge."

⇨ Reprimand in private.

⇨ Do not invite people who consistently cause problems.

FOCUS ON THE BEHAVIOR, NOT THE PERSON

It is so tempting to attack the person who seems to be throwing a wrench into anything positive the group is trying to accomplish. After all, they may be attacking others. If we choose this route, however, we may say or do things that we later regret. Worse, attacking people can have longer-term consequences.

When people are embroiled in verbal battles with others, it is difficult for them to rise above the fray. Here are some ways a facilitator might handle a disruptive confrontation between two or more people in a meeting by focusing on the behavior instead of the people:

⇨ Suggest a process for handling questions and concerns; this takes the burden off the people involved. For example, the facilitator might say something such as, "Time out, group. We want to make sure everybody's input is heard, and we'll make sure there is an opportunity to do that following the board's reports. Make a note of any questions or concerns you have, and we'll address them during the question and answer session."

⇨ Address the group and explain how shouting and interrupting is not going to accomplish anything. Suggest that each person take five minutes to write out his or her point of view. Then, give a chance to state their position,

without interruption from others. The silence created
by the writing exercise helps to calm things down and
to refocus the discussion.

⇨ If tensions and tempers are high, call for a break; approach the people involved in the fray and ask each
person to paraphrase the other's point of view. Out of
the "spotlight," this should help each to listen, and to
seek to understand the other.

UTILIZE GROUND RULES AS A NEUTRAL JUDGE

Once the group agrees to ground rules for meetings, such as "only
one person talk at a time," the facilitator and others can refer to them when
they are violated. Although it would be impossible to create a rule in
advance for every situation, there are a number of ground rules that serve
to remind group participants in advance of what is expected, and can be
invoked if necessary. See Chapter 4 for suggested ground rules.

REPRIMAND IN PRIVATE

Direct confrontations with people whose behavior is disruptive should
be done in private, away from other group members, whenever possible.
Staging a public "showdown" may be as disruptive as the original behavior itself, and could undermine a facilitator's ability to continue running
the meeting.

As noted previously, a comment directed to the group that reminds
them of specific ground rules may be all that is necessary to stop an
undesirable behavior. However, when someone or a small group of people
continue to "act out," a private conversation is appropriate. Call a break
and ask to meet with the people who are causing the disruption.

In private, the conversation can be direct and candid. Even so, it is
wise to remain calm and explain your point of view directly. The balanced
response technique can be useful in such situations. Start with pluses and
move to concerns. For example: "Geraldine, it is obvious you have many

ideas to contribute to this brainstorm session. The research you have done gives you a real edge, and we can all benefit from the preparation you have done. However, I need your help. I am concerned that we won't get the best thinking from the rest of the group if they aren't given a chance to contribute their ideas freely. When you interrupt people who are offering their ideas, they tend to close down and keep quiet. How can we get their best thinking and yours as well?" Inviting the person causing the problem to help solve it can be a powerful path to a solution.

Who should handle the conversation with people demonstrating disruptive behavior? The meeting initiator is probably the best choice, as he or she may exert more influence by their relationship to the offender.

Do Not Invite People Who Consistently Cause Problems

Sometimes the subtle approach just doesn't work. If someone consistently disrupts meetings, simply do not invite him or her to the next meeting, and tell the person why. This decision is up the meeting initiator, who is also obliged to tell the person why he or she is not being invited. Of course, if the offending person is the initiator or a senior executive, it would be difficult to use this approach. However, an outside facilitator may be able to confront the person one-on-one to point out how his or her behavior is affecting the efficiency of meetings.

Specific Disruptive Behaviors

Here are some several behaviors that can disrupt meetings, and suggested approaches for dealing with them.

Problem/Behavior	Symptom/Description	Possible Approaches
Habitual latecomer	Consistently late to meetings.	1) Start on time. After the meeting, ask privately why he or she is always so late. 2) For "first time offenders," suggest reading the group notes to catch up. 3) Ask him/her to facilitate next meeting.
Broken record	Repeats points already covered.	1) Refer to group notes: "We've already covered this. Alan, do you have anything new to add?" 2) Remind of the focus of meeting.
Side conversations	Whispered or louder conversations among two or more members.	1) Enforce ground rule of one meeting/one talk at a time. "Hey, folks—let's keep a single focus here." 2) Ask them to share their ideas with the group. 3) Separate the people. 4) Get up and walk around to participants. This will usually end their discussion.

War stories	Brings up anecdotes that may or may not be related to subject.	1) Remind person of the purpose of the meeting and the current focus or topic. 2) Approach person at the break. Point out how disruptive stories are for the group. 3) Glance at your watch. Use time urgency as a reason to cut the stories short.
Time waster	Asks questions that are covered in pre-meeting handout materials.	1) Gently remind him/her that the information is in the materials, and then move on to someone else. Ask how his or her points can help the group come to a solution.
Competitor	Vying with others to produce the best idea.	1) Remind group that idea generating is a team sport, and that all ideas are valid. Record the competitor's comments, and place them on the group memory with others.
Attention seeker	Talks loudly and often, dominating meeting.	1) Move toward the person, then shift focus to someone else. 2) Ask him/her to serve as recorder. 3) Confront directly at break or after.
Horsing around	Clowning, mimicking, disrupting group's work.	1) Approach at break and ask him or her to leave if not supportive of group.

Withdrawal	Drops out from active participation in meeting.	1) Ask their opinion on an issue. Be careful not to put on the spot—there may be a great idea brewing! 2) Break into small groups and pair shy people together. 3) Praise when they contribute.
Naysayers	Negates/puts down ideas of others.	Enforce ground rule to separate idea generation from evaluation. Introduce "building" language (Chapter 7).
Multitaskers	Check cell phone, PDA, or e-mail messages during the meeting.	1) Establish and enforce ground rule to turn all personal electronic devices off. 2) Ask them to check messages at the break.
Mr./Ms. Minutia	Brings up or dwells on small details not relevant to issue.	Suggest that the details/issues be set aside "for now" (in the parking lot), and schedule a time to cover them.
Sidetracker	Brings up new issues not related to current focus.	1) Put the issue in the parking lot and cover at end of meeting if time allows. 2) Suggest putting the issue on the agenda for the next meeting.

CHAPTER 14

USING TECHNOLOGY TO ENHANCE MEETINGS

The Truth You Often Hear

"What's that? Speak up, you're fading in and out."

...and the New Reality

"Be sure to check into the virtual meeting room by noon tomorrow with your comments and suggestions."

Technology-Enabled Meetings

This chapter concentrates on strategies and techniques for meetings that are supported or enabled electronically. There are many advantages to using technology to bring people together in meetings without getting on an airplane or even driving across town. When an organization has employees and clients in multiple locations, or employees and contractors working at home, the time and cost savings of electronic conferences compared to live meetings is significant. Even in the same office, the use of technology can often lead to more effective and productive mee

Telephone conference calls have been around for decades, and still represent the vast majority of "distributed" meetings, where participants are in more than one location. The Internet enables real time (synchronous) or asynchronous meetings to take place with dozens, hundreds, or even thousands of participants. A myriad of programs and tools is available for face-to-face and electronic meetings that enhance planning, inviting participants, collaboration, idea generation, note taking, and follow-up.

TELEPHONE CONFERENCE CALLS

The simplest kind of electronic meeting is a telephone conference, and the technology for small phone conferences is easy. Three-way calling allows several people to connect with others for an instant telephone conference from any location in the world. Larger phone conferences involve participants calling into a central number, or with one or more locations using conference room phones. Voice conference calls may also be conducted or enhanced by using the Internet (see next section). Telephone meetings can be highly productive if some basic principles and a few peculiarities are kept in mind.

For any phone meeting with four or more people, or one that will last more than 20 minutes, I strongly recommend that you follow the Four Ps of planning, as you would for any meeting: purpose, people, place, and preparation. Start by establishing a clear purpose for the call, asking: "What do we expect to accomplish?" or, "Why are we having this meeting?" Link the purpose to one or more outcomes, and prepare a time-bound, prioritized agenda that ties to the outcomes desired.

Keep the number of participants to a minimum. It is often difficult to keep track of who is talking if there is a large number of people on the line, or if everyone does know the other participants. For certain topics, it e for the initiator to hold a series of one-on-one larger group together in a conference call to sum-

Using Technology to Enhance Meetings

The "place" may seem inconsequential, because participants can call from virtually anywhere, but it is not. All participants should call in from places or conference rooms that are quiet, if at all possible. I was a participant in a phone conference recently during which one attendee called in from his cell phone in a busy airport. Flight announcements and the general noise level constantly interrupted our ability to concentrate on the issues. More than once a participant has called to a teleconference from a cell phone while driving in traffic. Not only is this practice dangerous, in one instance the rest of us were treated to a colorful litany of expletives when the caller was cut off by another driver!

Preparation is as critical for phone meetings as it is for in-person meetings. The start time, agenda, process, materials, and so on, should be planned thoroughly by the initiator or facilitator, and communicated to all participants.

Be sure to let conferees know exactly how they will join the meeting. Do they call in or will they be called? Will the originator set things up? Will a special pass code or PIN be required? Will an operator be involved in connecting? How far in advance of the meeting start time should each party join in?

With dozens of options available from third-party vendors for centralized conference calls, keep in mind that for three or four people, a conference call might be as easy as activating three-way calling from one or more of the phones.

Send the agenda and advance review materials to every participant before of the meeting, if possible. The facilitator or initiator may want to call or e-mail key participants to confirm agenda priorities. Send materials no more than a few days ahead of the conference; otherwise, they may get lost among other work materials. At the very minimum, go over the purpose and agenda at the start of the call.

Before discussing documents or other written materials, be sure all participants have copies, or can access them on a Website. The perso referring to the visual material should be very clear about which docu or graphic is being discussed, and confirm that all participants are "on the same page." Example: "Let's take a look now at chart number four dated June 18th, with the heading 'Trailing 12 months Operating Expenses.'"

When two or more people are using one phone in a room, a high-quality conference phone is helpful. Conference telephones vary widely in quality, and it is a smart idea to invest in a good system if you make many conference calls.

With more than five or six people, you may want to appoint a facilitator for the phone conference—usually just one of the participants. The facilitator maintains focus by working the agenda, adhering to time frames, and insuring participation from all group members. The facilitator should go around the room occasionally to be sure that all points of view are being heard, people have a chance to participate, and that everyone is still connected.

A facilitator or moderator to manage the proceedings is a must for larger conference calls, such as tele-seminars. When the discussion wanders from the agenda, the facilitator can intervene and suggest handling tangential issues at a later time. The parking lot technique (Chapter 5) is useful for such issues.

Because you can't read visual cues, participants should interject their speaking with frequent pauses, to allow other participants to join in with thoughts, ideas, and feedback. Many voices are similar, so each person speaking should identify him- or herself before beginning to speak, especially at the beginning of the meeting. I have found that for larger groups, it may be useful for the facilitator (and each participant) to draw a virtual room on a piece of paper, with stick figures and names to better track who is participating.

that extraneous noises such as whispering, paper
g, and typing on a computer keyboard are exagger-
ces. One of the most frequent complaints I hear in
ps is that conference call participants often multi-
in phone conference calls (see Chapter 13).

Appoint one person to act as recorder, to capture and later summarize key discussion points, decisions, and action items. Because other participants will not be able to see the group notes during the phone conference, the facilitator or recorder should summarize action items verbally at the end of the call, and by e-mail afterward.

If a phone conference is essentially "one-way," that is, one person talking and others listening for a period of time, invite listeners to activate the mute buttons on their phones to minimize noise on the call. When it is time for feedback, participants can simply deactivate the mute button and begin talking.

If you meet frequently with the same group by telephone conference, spend a few minutes every few weeks debriefing your phone meetings, noting what works and what might be improved.

WEB CONFERENCING

Resources for setting up conference calls are readily available on the Internet, and the technology is beginning to supplement or even replace voice conferences using telephone lines. There are dozens of third-party service providers that can be found easily with a Google search. A typical menu of services might include dial-in conferencing through regular phone lines or audio conferencing through VOIP (Voice Over Internet Protocol) on the Web, "always open" conference (chat) rooms, or the ability to share visuals, screen shots, applications, and video. Services are priced on a per-minute/per-participant rate or a flat monthly fee. Most will let you try the service or program for a free trial period.

Collaboration tools, often known as groupware, enable participants to view and edit documents, presentations, and drawings from remote locations, and to participate in surveys. These tools can be used in real time or in asynchronous meetings, where people are invited to participate at their convenience. Such tools are an excellent means to enable people to contribute ideas and reach consensus, often without having to meet at the same time. Web-based tools are especially useful for getting input, ideas, and consensus from large, disbursed groups.

As of this writing, several vendors have developed impressive programs featuring enhanced audio that enables participants to converse in real time, share multimedia content, use interactive whiteboards, take surveys or quizzes, and a number of other features.

Be sure that all participants have a high-speed Internet connection, and the necessary software, if required. One nice aspect of Web-based collaboration tools is that usually no software is needed, minimizing the chance of possible hardware or platform conflicts.

Facilitators (in some cases a technical or IT person) should know the technology inside and out, to enable accommodation and orientation of new participants, rapid tabulation of results, and how to deal with glitches. The meeting should focus on the agenda and purpose, not the technology.

Many Web-based meetings include online chats, which can be done with or without voice communication. Although the absence of nuance via body language, vocal intonation, and group reaction may be an issue, an online chat conference can be an efficient way to gather data or generate ideas. Recently, I facilitated an online focus group with 12 people in remote locations. The purpose was to get reactions from consumers on advertising concepts. We used a group shareware program that enabled participants to view visuals (mock ads and concept statements) on a Website, enter their reactions anonymously in a live chat room, rate their preferences with an online tool, and then discuss their reasons and impressions with the moderator by a telephone voice line, which was kept open for the entire session.

Videoconference Meetings

The last step up the ladder of electronic meetings is videoconferences. We have come a long way since AT&T first introduced the Picturephone at the 1964 World's Fair in New York. Videoconferences are growing in popularity, as the cost of equipment and connection time has almost become a non-issue. The advantage of video-conferencing is obvious: each participant can see everyone else and converse in real time. The strategies and tips for phone conferences apply to videoconferences, as well as a few others.

For several decades, videoconferencing has been available to those who could afford it, and the quality of such video meetings has continuously improved. With high-speed Internet connections, anyone who wants to hold a video meeting with reasonable quality can do so with relatively little expense. For meetings of two or three, at least one vendor (Skype) is a free videoconference service.

For distributed meetings with six or fewer participants, the next step is to use any one of a number of applications that enable low-cost videoconferences. Each participant must have access to a computer with a videocam at his or her desktop or laptop. Most newer computers have videocams built in (or available as an inexpensive add-on), which makes this option even more affordable. The software programs I have reviewed enable participants to view others in individual windows or in other screen configurations. If visual aids are used, they should be simple, as participants will have much to look at on their screens. Even better—send the visual material or documents by e-mail prior to the conference, so participants can review in advance and then refer to their own copies during the video meeting.

If the program or connection produces jerky images (similar to watching an old movie), participants should slow things down and speak clearly so that everyone can track the discussion.

Meeting Management Software

Software, such as MeetingSense, is available that provides tools for meeting initiators, facilitators, and participants to streamline the planning, note-taking, and follow-up of meetings. The best of the packages enables users to invite participants (including linking to Microsoft Outlook), clarify the meeting purpose, distribute advance preparation materials, record decisions and action items in real time, and send summaries, action steps, and follow-up reminders to all participants and other interested parties. Meeting management software can be used effectively to support real-time live meetings, telephone conferences, and videoconferences.

Additional Thoughts on Electronic Meetings

Despite the ability to connect electronically with virtually anyone in the world, meetings are still interactions between two or more individuals. Be careful of getting too swept up in the gadgets and toys, and losing sight of the basic elements of planning and running meetings that matter: purposeful, focused, and action-oriented.

When people who normally meet by phone, Web, or videoconference get together face to face, I have observed that the dynamics change dramatically. Nuances that are lost in etherspace are noticed, body language and eye contact take on more importance, and "water cooler" sidebars come into play. For this reason alone, I recommend that people who usually meet electronically strive to meet in person at least once a year, in an environment that allows some social interaction as well. It will make a difference.

CHAPTER 15

ONE-ON-ONE MEETINGS

The Truth You Never Hear

"Hi, John. Come on in—you can watch me make a few phone calls while we pretend to have a meeting."

The Challenges

⇨ Unscheduled "drop-in" meetings can disrupt schedules and concentration. A series of spur-of-the-moment meetings can ruin your whole day.

⇨ Without a purpose or agenda, ground rules, or time management, one-on-one meetings can easily wander into free-flowing conversations that chew up time and ultimately accomplish little.

⇨ If a one-on-one meeting takes place in the office of one of the participants, there is a "home court" advantage that can impact the discussion. The president of one company for which I worked had pewter models of bar-racudas prominently displayed on his desk. Although they did fit his personality, the presence of the barracu-das (baring their teeth) certainly set a tone for any meet-ing held in his office.

⇨ Phone calls, e-mail alerts, and other distractions can quickly change the focus of one-to-one meetings, and do not respect the time of the other person.

⇨ Without agreement on action items, one-on-one meet-ings might fall short of achieving any meaningful results.

Strategies and Ideas for One-on-One Meetings

⇨ Always schedule one-on-one meetings in advance and allow (or initiate) impromptu meetings only when they are short and absolutely necessary.

⇨ Establish a clear purpose and time parameters.

⇨ Schedule one-on-ones in a neutral setting.

⇨ Send all phone calls to voice mail, and turn off e-mail alerts.

⇨ Always end with agreement on action steps.

ALWAYS SCHEDULE ONE-ON-ONES IN ADVANCE

One-on-one exchanges come in many flavors and styles. They range from informal, impromptu chats in the hallway to highly structured inter-views, presentations, and formal performance reviews. Most casual con-versations, including phone calls, do not count as meetings, in the traditional sense. Certainly, if there is a sense of urgency and you need to get a quick opinion or decision from someone, a spontaneous one-on-one meeting can occur. If you are the initiator of such a meeting, at least ask the other person if they have five minutes for (your topic).

Any one-on-one exchange that is expected to take more than five minutes should be scheduled in advance. This applies to telephone meetings as well as face-to-face exchanges. The two people meeting should protect that time on their calendars, as they would for any important meeting.

If you find that spontaneous meetings chew up significant portions of your day and distract you from concentrating on other priorities, establish "no interruption" periods when you are in your office. Allow no one to drop in and start a meeting during these times, unless there is truly a crisis. Be sure to allow open times, when you are available for discussions and unplanned meetings.

If any of your associates set no-interruption times, be sure to honor their request!

Establish a Clear Purpose and Time Parameters

When scheduling a one-on-one, establish the purpose with the other person. When the meeting starts, restate it so you are both clear on what you expect to accomplish. Example: "Hal, I want to review the key findings from the third quarter customer survey with you, and to suggest two actions we need to take in the next few weeks."

Once both people agree on the purpose, they should also agree on the time, even if there is only one agenda item. It can be something as simple as saying: "Let's plan for 10 minutes." Meetings of this type often do not require detailed agendas, unless it is a more formal discussion, such as a sales presentation, project update, or performance review.

Although managing time in one-on-ones is similar to any other meeting, both people are usually actively engaged in the discussion, and it is easy for time to slip away. Paying attention to the clock does not allow you to focus fully on the conversation. Have you ever noticed how uncomfortable you feel whenever a person with whom you are talking keeps looking at their watch? A better way to end on time and stay focused on each other is to use an electronic timer (most cell phones and PDAs have this feature) to set an alarm for the end time, or a few minutes before. When the alarm sounds, bring the meeting to a quick conclusion. If you need more time, agree with the other person to extend it for a specified length; reset the timer and continue.

Because there are fewer agenda items, one-on-ones are usually more focused than larger meetings. However, because they are often more casual, it is easy to stray from the purpose and wander off into other topics. This requires both participants to be attentive to the issue at hand, and to suggest a refocus when necessary.

Hold One-on-One Meetings in a Neutral Location

If possible, schedule longer one-on-one meetings in some place other than either participant's office. This will ensure that there is no "home court advantage" because of the subtle trappings and other symbols of an office. I know one executive who always insists on having meetings with subordinates in his office. This person is "vertically challenged" and the chair behind his desk has been raised so that he always looks down on all but the tallest people who enter his space. The fact that everyone knows the "game" makes it a bit absurd, of course.

If you must meet in an office, use the conference table if there is one. Otherwise, move the chairs so there is not a desk separating you, if there is space.

Send All Phone Calls to Voice Mail and Turn Off E-mail Alerts

There are few things more irritating than to be in a one-on-one meeting with someone who responds to a chiming cell phone or ringing desk phone. In my work as a group chair with Vistage International, I have one-on-one meetings with approximately 24 executives each month. When we both remember to turn off cell phones and let desk phone calls go to voice mail, the meetings are far more focused and productive. I must admit that

I have often forgotten to silence my cell phone, only to have it interrupt the meeting at a crucial point, even if I don't answer it.

Computers that sound an alert whenever a new e-mail message is received are fairly benign, unless the recipient stops the one-on-one discussion to read. We are equipped with so many electronic tools that it is difficult to remember to disengage them all whenever we are meeting with others. However, giving each other full attention results in a more focused and productive meeting.

END WITH CLEAR ACTION STEPS

Because one-on-ones are usually more casual than other meetings, it is easy to just end the discussion with no clear-cut follow-up or action steps. Don't let this happen in your one-on-ones—always confirm any decisions made, then recap the next steps: who will do what, by when.

APPENDIX

Meeting Planning Guide and Template

Idea-Generation Meeting Summary

Meeting Effectiveness Checklist Template

Meeting Effectiveness Checklist Sample

Meeting Planning Guide and Template

CLARIFY TYPE AND PURPOSE

⇨ Specify the TYPE of meeting (Information/Advisory. Creative/Idea Generation, Decision-making, Problem-solving, Training/Learning, Negotiating).

⇨ NAME the meeting according to its primary purpose, issue, or outcome.

⇨ State PURPOSE of meeting: what you want to accomplish; the primary issue, event, or process that will define the focus of the meeting.

⇨ State the LOCATION of the meeting.

⇨ Specify the DATE, DURATION, and START/END TIME of the meeting.

⇨ Designate MEETING INITIATOR (person calling the meeting), FACILITATOR (responsible for running the meeting), TIMEKEEPER, and RECORDER.

⇨ Name a CONTACT person—someone to accept confirmations and handle other logistics.

⇨ List intended meeting OUTCOMES. Start each with an action verb: decide, finish, agree, and so on.

DEVELOP PRELIMINARY AGENDA, PROCESS, AND RESOURCES REQUIRED

⇨ List potential topics or agenda items; either solicit from participants or meeting owner/facilitator decide. Each agenda item should relate to the meeting purpose, state an intended outcome, and have a time estimate.

⇨ List the PARTICIPANTS whose presence is required (M = must be present; S = should be present). Consider inviting some for a portion of the meeting

⇨ Clarify the process to be employed for each agenda item. Examples:
- Open discussion
- Presentation + Q&A
- Breakouts, small groups
- Exercises or other activities
- Structured discussion—round robin, time limit

⇨ Identify the information, reports, and other resources required for the meeting.

CONSTRUCT THE FINAL PRIORITIZED AGENDA

⇨ Start with the most important item/topic and its estimated time; add subsequent items/topics in order of priority.

⇨ Leave five to 10 minutes at end for parking lot items, admin. issues, set next date, and so on.

⇨ Plan to the time allocated for the meeting.

PUBLISH AGENDA AND
ASSIGN PRE-MEETING "HOMEWORK"

⇨ Publish the prioritized agenda to all participants in advance of the meeting.

⇨ Include instructions for pre-meeting reading, departmental input, and other preparation requested of participants.

⇨ Ask participants to confirm (R.S.V.P.) their attendance to the contact person.

MEETING PLANNING TEMPLATE

Type and Purpose

Type:
Meeting name:
Meeting purpose:
Location:
Date:
Duration:
Start time:
End time:
Meeting initiator:
Facilitator:
Recorder:
Timekeeper
Contact person:
Meeting outcomes:

-
-
-

Develop Preliminary Agenda, Process, and Resources Required

- Topic
   Process
   Estimated time
   Participants
- Topic
   Process
   Estimated time
   Participants
- Topic
   Process
   Estimated time
   Participants

- Information, reports, resources required.

Construct the Final Prioritized Agenda

- Rank previous items in order of priority: most important topic/item first.

Publish agenda and assign pre-meeting "homework"

- Print out and send agenda with attachments or instructions for pre-meeting preparation. Ask participants to confirm attendance with contact person.

MEETING MINUTES TEMPLATE

Company/Organization:
Department/Team/Committee:
Meeting Initiator:
Date/Time:

Meeting Date & Location:< Date of Meeting > < Location >
Meeting Purpose:< Stated purpose of meeting >
Facilitator & Recorder:< Meeting Facilitator > < Meeting Recorder >
Copy to all participants plus:< Additional recipients >

Participants:	

Meeting Minutes & Action Summary

Agenda Item:

Presenter or Discussion Leader:

Key Conclusions/Summary of Discussion & Decisions:

- Brief summary of conclusions and decisions.
- Detailed recap of discussions leading up to conclusions not necessary.

Action Items

What will be done	Who will do it	By when

Agenda Item:

Presenter or Discussion Leader:

Key Conclusions/Summary of Discussion & Decisions:

- Brief summary of conclusions and decisions.
- Detailed recap of discussions leading up to conclusions not necessary.

Action Items

What will be done	Who will do it	By when

(Repeat as necessary for additional agenda items)

Appendix

Idea-Generation Meeting Summary

Meeting Date & Location:< Date of Meeting > < Location >
Meeting Purpose:< Stated purpose of meeting >
Facilitator & Recorder:< Meeting Facilitator > < Meeting Recorder >
Copy to all participants plus:< Additional recipients >

Participants:	

Meeting Results & Action Summary

Initial problem (issue, challenge) stated:
Problem/issue/challenge as redefined:
Initial thought-starters and ideas

- List headline or brief description of each idea or thought-starter.
- Idea number two.
- Idea number three, and so on.

Top ideas/solutions selected by group for further refinement or consideration:

- List "winning" ideas selected by group in as much detail as necessary to.
- Idea/Solution two.
- Idea/Solution three, and so on.

Action Items

What will be done	Who will do it	By when

Meeting Effectiveness Checklist Template

Group_____ Date_____Purpose_____

Rate the effectiveness of today's meeting, using a scale of 1 to 5 (1 = great, 5 = lousy)	Rating	Additional Comments: please be as specific as possible
Overall effectiveness		
Accomplished our purpose		
Right people in attendance throughout		
Meeting room worked for our purpose		
Participants came prepared to discuss agenda		
Agenda developed and communicated		
Meeting stay on track/ focused throughout		
Presentations well organized and delivered		

Facilitation effective		
Used positive feedback methods		
Reached consensus		
We had fun		
Action steps assigned		
Started on time		
Ended on time		
What else can we do to improve effectiveness		

Meeting Effectiveness Checklist Sample

Group: Benefits Task Force **Date:** Mar. 14 **Purpose:** New ideas for benefits

Rate the effectiveness of today's meeting, using a scale of 1 to 5 (1 = great, 5 = lousy)	Rating	Additional Comments: please be as specific as possible
Overall effectiveness	2	Better than last two sessions
Accomplished our purpose	1	Really productive
Right people in attendance throughout	1	Group has come together
Meeting room worked for our purpose	3	Air conditioning needs fixing!
Participants came prepared to discuss agenda	2	Most read survey/ had ideas
Agenda developed and communicated	1	Clear

Meeting stay on tracked/ focused throughout	3	Wandered off a few times
Presentations well organized and delivered	2	Only one—Jan did her homework
Facilitation effective	3	We are all improving
Used positive feedback methods	3	Need to work on bal. response
Reached consensus	3	Resorted to voting on one issue
We had fun	1	
Action steps assigned	1	Thanks to Sandi for volunteering
Started on time	3	Ten minutes late starting
Ended on time	1	Yes!
What else can we do to improve effectiveness	Send out review materials before each meeting	

INDEX

Index

ABOUT THE AUTHOR

Charlie Hawkins is a recognized expert in the area of interpersonal and small group communications. He is president of Seahawk Associates, a management consulting firm based in Albuquerque, New Mexico. In addition to his work as a strategic planning facilitator and speaker, he runs three business round table groups as a chair for Vistage International, the world's leading organization for business owners, company presidents, and CEOs.

Earlier in his business management career, Charlie was vice president, marketing services for Dr Pepper Company, and held marketing positions with Procter & Gamble, Mennen Company, and Sunshine Biscuits. He was also founder and president of a marketing communications firm in Dallas, Texas. From 1989 through 2001, he designed and facilitated presentation skills seminars for more than 2,000 MBA candidates at the University of Chicago Graduate School of Business. Charlie holds an MBA in marketing from Columbia University (New York) and a BA in communications from Florida State University.

He lives in Albuquerque with his wife, Alicia. They have two grown children and four grandchildren.

Make Meetings Matter

To learn more about Seahawk Associates, visit *www.charliehawkins.com*. If you'd like to contact Charlie directly, he can be reached at (888)285-HAWK (4295), or Charlie@charliehawkins.com.